Am I judgmental
if I say you're judgmental?

Invitation Publishing

Am I
Judgmental
If I Say You're
Judgmental?

by Rohail Aslam

Everyone's problem
that nobody knows about

For Mum, Dad and their bravery.

My life can change my words.
My words can change my life.

Am I judgmental if I say you're judgmental?
By Rohail Aslam

First edition published June 2021

INVITATION PUBLISHING LTD
512-514 Berridge Road West
Nottingham
NG7 5JU

Tel: +44[0] 115 8550961
E-mail: info@invitationpublishing.co.uk
https://www.invitationpublishing.co.uk

Distributed by INVITATION PUBLISHING LTD.

Cataloguing-in-Publication Data is available from the British Library.

ISBN: 9781902248929

Typeset in Minion Pro.

Illustrations by Rohail Aslam

Design by Nottingham Printers and Signs

Contents

Foreword

This timely book takes us on a journey of how we can judge without the potential pitfalls of being judgmental. Although the book makes its own judgements about the world and its flaws, the key message of how we should be using the art of being judgmental is very clear. Whilst some level of being judgmental might be necessary to draw lines of what might be considered moral or fair, it is the manner and form of this judgement that seems to be the crux of the problem and lies at the heart of the message from this book. Using an accessible and conversational style, Rohail explores what being judgmental means and how it manifests in different ways, particularly its more malevolent and destructive forms, and how judgmentalism has 'interlaced itself culturally within the fabric of just about every society on the planet'.

Rohail enables the reader to deconstruct what being judgmental entails on an everyday and personal level, using helpful metaphors to explain and interrogate the quality of our judgements and the impact of these. He manages to contextualise how making judgements as such is not necessarily something to avoid at all costs. He distinguishes between the importance of, and sometimes need to make, sound and valid judgements from the act of being judgmental, which seeks to blame and diminish, to belittle and dominate. In this way, he shows how complex the notion of judgmentalism is and highlights the unfortunate consequences of being judgmental on our relationships and behaviours, often leading to negative outcomes and 'unhappy and dysfunctional environments'. He explores the 'covert and illusive' nature of being judgmental to help us make fair and balanced judgements that seek positive outcomes and aim to restore, whilst avoiding the pitfalls of harsh judgements that have negative intent and are filled with condemnation.

He draws on personal views and opinions to illustrate the everyday way we all exercise judgement in both positive and negative ways. He shows how judgmental conduct 'pervades all cultures, languages, faiths and nationalities' and in doing so, illustrates how judgmentalism can be utilised for the common good. In doing so, he notes how not being judgmental enough can yield its own problems, often leading to passive or misguided acceptance of unhelpful and unjust behaviours, or a world with no boundaries and anarchic interpretations of 'anything goes', or perceived infringements of individual rights that are unbalanced by a sense of responsibility and social justice. In this way, he shows how we still need to challenge and assess circumstances, behaviours and values to create a fairer world, using judgement for a positive moral purpose.

Another bonus of this book is the way Rohail has cleverly integrated the concepts of judgement within the process of emotion coaching to illustrate how emotion coaching can support our ability to transcend the barriers of being judgmental and communicate more effectively with others. He shows how this can enable us to make more appropriate and often necessary judgements, such as setting limits on certain behaviours. He provides practical tips and illustrations of how we can communicate in more empathic and less judgmental ways that can cross age, culture and gender boundaries. As such, he brings to light the many ways and forms being judgmental takes but most importantly offers a practical and helpful way to change how we engage with others and improve the quality of our judgmental interactions. With emotion coaching we can create more 'calm, connecting and cooperative' ways of communicating that will de-escalate difficult situations and 'pull back the reins of confrontation'. Drawing on his wealth of knowledge of working with and supporting 'troubled' children and families, he offers a fresh perspective on how we can address some of the most significant issues of our time. He calls on us to start a 'non-judgmental revolution' and shows us how emotion coaching can help us to judge without being judgmental and become more 'humble humans', as Rohail so eloquently puts it.

Dr Janet Rose, co-founder Emotion Coaching UK

Introduction

I t's now June 2020 as I write this. The Coronavirus lockdown has been in effect for around four months and the world, the people, their social norms, their livelihoods and most of all their emotional health has and continues to take an unprecedented beating. From the moment words like 'virus,' 'contagious,' 'social distancing,' 'stay home, 'self-isolate' and 'daily death toll' began to circulate in the media, people everywhere had yet another plethora of emotional battles to deal with on-top of everything else.

So little surprise to see the statistics of domestic violence and abuse sky-rocket globally, less surprise than that to watch the last 8 minutes and 46 seconds of a black man's life trigger a global backlash against racism in all its forms and least surprise of all to hear the indignant self-preserving voices of western leaders, devoid of empathy, vowing to stamp out all and any efforts to change this paradigm of racist supremacy.

It's at this point this year, when the lockdown hit, that my work in Emotion Coaching had really begun to broaden. Emotion Coaching is a way of engaging with one another in order to enhance our relationships, our emotional and physical health. It is the culmination of more than four decades of research by world leading Developmental Psychologist Dr John Gottman of the Gottman Institute in the US, whose book 'Raising an emotionally intelligent child' I read in 2015. A book that completely transformed the work I was doing with children and families with emotional and behavioural difficulties. So just before the lockdown, I had started to expand my work in delivering training sessions to parents, school staff and even in the private sector. Supporting people to start discovering the potential in learning about and harnessing their own emotional behaviour, then watching how their own changes triggered the same in others around them. I even resigned from my full-time teaching job in a school in order to devote more time to this work.

And then within days, the lockdown happened. It stopped this work dead, and the irony was, that now was the time people needed this guidance more than ever; now was the time everyone needed to learn some essential skills in handling confrontations at home, in how to get their kids to continue studying when the schools had closed their gates; in how to keep themselves calm and focussed in the face of unemployment and deep uncertainty about what the future holds for us all.

Furthermore, we all know how the fall-out from a crisis can often be longer, more painful than the crisis itself, and reflection on this sobering thought opens up a whole new chasm of seemingly inevitable effects. Like the impact of the lockdown on our children's education, on the confidence of our skilled workforces, on all the bereaved, on all the jobless breadwinners, on the employers who must somehow continue to swim.

So, my first and pretty natural reaction was one of complete defeat. That was it! My work had stopped. The schools had closed shop and so I'd now need to wait it out. However, this was followed instantly by the fact that it was now more than ever that this wisdom and support needed to get out there, everywhere and in as many different languages as possible. So that's what I set out to do.

It's this turning point that began to transform my work from face to face, to being delivered completely on-line. It was pretty obvious and completely natural that the internet was fast to become the closest and most critical friend to anyone and any organisation during this completely unchartered time. However, it's also at this point that I had started to really reflect on where in my work I felt I must start to focus more. What (as this lockdown rolled out and the world began to grapple with the fall-out), were the most difficult challenges we were all facing in how we engaged with one another? What were the reasons for this instant knee-jerk spike in domestic abuse and even murder? OK, we were all suddenly chickens in a coop, and the thought of spending all day everyday with each other without respite was a challenge in itself, but even in supposedly 'normal' families, where there is no known history of domestic abuse, people were and are still feeling like getting through even one day without a confrontation is pretty unrealistic.

So, I was hell-bent on trying to boil it down to something. That one toxic element that lies at the root of not just some but all conflict, and it's this process of trying to simplify it all that brought me to the imposing and seemingly impenetrable gates of Judgmentalism; impenetrable because as I began to reflect on the incalculable range of conflicts relentlessly unfolding in our world every moment, everywhere, it appeared to me that each and every single conflict I read about or saw on a screen or witnessed or even imagined, anywhere, was, at its source, triggered by an act of judgmentalism. By somebody judging someone else based more on prejudices, misconceptions, preconceptions and desires to upstage, demean or control the other, rather than wanting to problem solve, avoid a confrontation, and even teach the other something valuable and meaningful. The end goal is all too often not one of harmony but one of war. Be it at home between family members or a government's round table, a judgmental response is almost always our first 'go to' choice of response.

It seemed clear, therefore, that it was this word and all that this word implies; it was this word that I needed to explore. I had already heard it batted around almost every conference, meeting or training session I had attended about relationships, child development or communication. However never was this word brought to the fore ground and singled out as being any more complicit in all our sorrows than anything else. This impression only became deeper and more prominent as I explored this further, particularly when I began to reflect on how practically plausible it is to think of responses that are not judgmental and thereby, in an instant, could avoid a confrontation or a kick-off.

Perhaps another reason why the word judgmental hasn't been put under the surgeon's spotlight anywhere near enough, is because it's more often a word that we only seem to associate with religious teachings. Later in this book, we look at what the different faiths say about judgmentalism, which is rather a lot. My job now, however, is to drag this word kicking, screaming and frothing at the mouth out of the shadows and into the broad light of day, so we can try to get to the bottom of it all.

Despite all my apprehensions about the current predicament of mankind, I believe that as our knowledge is increasing about the mind, the emotions and their power to navigate our overall health and relationships, the human race is fast approaching the threshold of its next evolutionary step. I hope. A step that sees us all realising how to master our communication with one another, how to focus on a higher common purpose when choosing our words with each other, and ultimately blowing those impenetrable gates off their hinges.

This book sets out to first explore the theory that it is indeed judgmentalism that we all need to give some serious thought to right now if we're to cross that threshold into a more loving world, and if it is, then how are we going to do it?

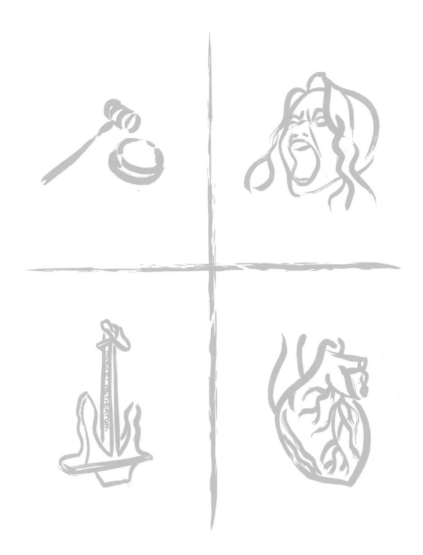

CHAPTER 1:

The Dreaded Judge!

To judge is a practice that comes as naturally to us all as taking a breath. It is one of our default mechanisms; an instant response to anything we sense, anything that others say or do. We shape an impression and then simply respond.

However, I'd first like to define the cataclysmic difference between making a judgment and being judgmental because a truly alarming number of people get quite confused with this. Let's take a regular day in any of our lives. A day that invariably consists of numerous judgments we need to make in order to function from the moment we open our eyes to the moment we drift off to sleep, like what we're going to eat, how much we're going to eat, what we're going to wear, how fast we're going to drive and so on. These are all based on tiny little risk assessments we have to make about what's good for us or not good for us. This is also described as 'healthy judgmental behaviour', where we point out actions or words that could be proven to be harmful to others.

It also dates back to our cave-man days according to Dr Audrey Tang, a chartered psychologist, lecturer and author, who says 'it goes back to the dawn of civilisation – humans being a collective that work best when members of any given tribe look out for one another. Humans are social creatures who do well when they collaborate. It was safer for us to move in tribes, and any outlier was seen as a potential threat.'

However, to be judgmental, as the dictionary states, is to 'have or display an overly critical point of view.' Being judgmental is when we're telling someone that they're stupid, when we open our mouths or raise our fists to ruin someone else's day in order to make ourselves feel momentarily better.

They say money is the root of all evil. I say being judgmental takes that accolade and runs way way off into the distance leaving only a cloud of dust. However, the plot thickens further when we reflect on the force that shapes those very impressions - the colossal backdrop of our own life's journey so far; a complex montage of memories, decisions, strokes of luck, battles, tragedies, successes, prejudices, passions, perceptions, fixations, epiphanies and, many of us believe, a spattering of good old divine inspiration from the creator!

The epic of each of our lives is there every moment in the form of neurological imprints in our brains, collectively and perpetually influencing each and every single impression we form of everything and everyone!

It is safe to say, therefore, that our life's trajectory is plotted out and signposted by these very judgments. Judgments that will lead us down any infinite combination of outcomes, and that's all on top of the fact that we are all born with a certain amount of pre-determined personality, a block of genetic coding issued to us whether we like it or not. Coding that has already made us fiery, or cool, or a mix of both or more even before we see the light of day. A code that may have already prescribed to us many of the basic elements of the people we will become, from our physiological profile right through to our temperament, our likes and dislikes, our sexuality and our instinctual interests.

However, once our judgment is made, it is surely the response we issue that determines the outcome of not only how we will feel, but also how the receiver will in turn respond to us. This suggests the need for a response that may not accurately reflect our judgment. Moreover, it also suggests that our response is more important than the judgment we formed, a judgment that was shaped and perhaps even distorted by the backdrop of our past experiences as mentioned above.

An example is when mother and son are in a confrontation, the son blurts out something very unkind in his anger. The mother's impression is that her son is rude and should be made to acknowledge his mistake, perhaps even be prepared to face a sanction for his behaviour. However, if she expresses these very words as she has felt them, it will most likely escalate the confrontation further. The mother wants to teach her son to change his behaviour in that moment as well as in the future. So instead she chooses to respond in a different way. In a way that allows her to connect with her son and guide him towards realising and acknowledging his mistake himself instead of spelling it out to him. She may say "I can see that you must be feeling really frustrated and angry, otherwise you would never speak to me like that. I really want to help you solve your problem so when you're feeling calmer may be we can talk then."

Here, the mother judges her son's behaviour, then chooses a way to respond to him that is designed more towards de-escalating the confrontation and getting the desired response from him than simply expressing exactly what she thinks of his behaviour.

This momentary processing from judgment to response that we face in our lives all day, every day, is the key factor that determines the outcomes of all of our interactions with the world around us. For it is this failure, or refusal to think enough before we respond, to be careless in forming a response before it is issued, that results everyday everywhere, in people of all ages conflicting with one another. We all know that the refusal to reflect on a thoughtful response is a much easier resort in the heat of the moment. The instant knee-jerk reaction of the reptilian brain has always and will always be the catalyst for unrest and misunderstanding in every setting. From all domestic homes, and workplaces, right up to 'the oval offices' of our world, children, parents and presidents are still in the dark about the potential in thinking before we 'open our trap!'

Am I judgmental if I say you're judgmental?

It seems clear initially that to point out to someone else that they are behaving judgmentally obviously requires one to be judgmental themselves. This is a conundrum that I love wrestling with! I revel in seeing it batted around on-line and it's reassuring (and even amusing) to see how people are trying to build a framework of meaning and definition around it. This moulding of what's judgmental and what isn't is still going on because I believe to this day, there has always been an ambiguity around it; partly because, the more of our days we spend being naturally judgmental, the less able we are to recognise when we're not being judgmental. So the already muddied waters of this book's title question will never clear until we all start to make the intention to change our responses to others, all day every day. And just like kicking an age-old habit, it can only happen in small steps. As the neuroscientist Dr Joe Dispenza explains, the way you decide to think and feel can affect the outer world. It's a process of gaining knowledge and then practice. Then, as you see small steps of progress, you start to pay attention to how you're also changing inside. How the positive effects of your changes are making you feel internally. That's when you simply continue repeating the new behaviours to continue feeling that way – and hey presto! The brain starts re-wiring the new 'you!'

From my own work and experience of dealing with judgmentalism and through gradually incorporating Emotion Coaching behaviours into my life, I've come to the conclusion that there are actually very clear ways to convey your feelings and opinions to someone without being negatively judgmental. Or at least not letting them feel that you're being judgmental. This is done easily by first connecting emotionally with them, bringing them closer to you through empathy and validation of their feelings.

That's even if you know or suspect straight away that they were in the wrong. You see, if you simply blurt out that thought at the start, then that's you being the dreaded judge, making them feel belittled and patronised. So, you prioritise their feelings first and establish the listeners role. It's only then, once they feel that you accept and respect how they feel, that they are so much more ready to acknowledge any short-coming of their own or to come up with a solution to their problem. They'll also know that you helped them towards the solution, which only strengthens your relationship, but they will still be left with the sense of achievement that ultimately, they came up with the solution. This is because, although you knew the answer to their problem, you guided them towards coming up with the solution themselves through this combination of connecting, empathising, then asking them questions that would help them to arrive at the answer. Dr Gottman's research has proven that kids whose parents engage with them using this or formulas like it, invariably start to learn how to problem solve independently. The holy grail of parenting!! But we'll look in detail at what this style of communication looks like later in the book, as well as how Emotion Coaching works just as effectively between adults too.

In the first part of this chapter, we see that we turn our judgments into responses and depending on how carefully we have thought out the responses, we will either succeed or fail in our endeavour. But what is the problem with being judgmental? To explore this, let's look at a few textbook examples of being judgmental:

A teacher points to a pupil in front of the class and says "That was a very rude thing to say! You ought to be ashamed of yourself!" We can see that the response the teacher gave to the child's behaviour was exactly what she judged. There was little or no reflection first on how else she could respond in order to connect with the child and teach them something.

This response triggers an escalation in the child's behaviour, who responds with "Don't care! It was Sam's fault! I hate your lesson anyway!" When we look at the child's response and explore how else the teacher could have responded and possibly helped the child to realise and even acknowledge his wrong doing himself, we can see how important it is to avoid judgmental statements.

If we think about how the Teacher could have done things differently, she could have begun by first getting the child alone instead of confronting him in front of others. She could then have focussed on connecting with him first, asking him why he had felt the need to use such language. Then, when he told her, she could have empathised with him, getting him on her side first, validating his emotions first, before asking him about the part he played in the incident. For its only when we connect with them first that they will then be prepared to admit their own wrongdoing or start thinking of solutions to their problem.

A wife returns home from work after having a tough day at the office and is looking and feeling quite stressed. She enters the kitchen where her son is busy helping himself to far too much chocolate spread on his toast. He's not even used a plate and is preparing his snack directly on the not too clean worktop surface. His mother instantly bellows at him from the doorway shouting "Jack! You just don't listen to a word I say about how much of that rubbish you eat! And again, you just can't be bothered to use a plate! That's a Playstation ban until tomorrow!" Jack, caught in the act, glares back at his mother and shouts "I was hungry and there were no more plates in the cupboard! You're always shouting at me! You never shout at Jane!" The husband walks into the kitchen after hearing the raised voices and glaring at his wife says 'Here we go again. You come back from work and every single day you're in a bad mood, nagging at all of us because of stuff that's happening somewhere else! I want you to just keep your emotional baggage at work! Don't bring it home because it's not our fault!"

This scene is a relentless exchange between three family members, completely devoid of empathy, and the really bad news is that 'empathy free' zones just like this one described are far more prevalent in most households the world over than households where people actually speak to each other thoughtfully and lovingly.

So why are we so quick to judge?

I believe there are a few reasons for this:
It is a 'no brainer!' It is clearly down to an innate egotistical hunger (and I know you'll agree with me when I say it's a ravenous one!) that we all have to be the one 'in the right;' to prove the other wrong! What is it about this hunger to upstage the other, to trip them up, to be the one to convey the bad news and burst their bubble, to be the first to put our finger on the all-important detail they overlooked, then magnanimously offer them help in solving their problem with one of those glowing, gloating yet ever so subtle smirks on our face. Sigmund Freud defined the Ego as being a force split into three parts: the id, the ego and the super ego. The id (Latin for 'it') is the chaotic part of the personality that drives much of our instinctual behaviour like our libido. The super ego is the moral conscience, and the ego is the part of our personality that mediates between the other two. However, regardless of how we define and breakdown

our ego, we all clearly see that it can regularly get us in to trouble when it goes unchecked.

Another reason why I believe we jump to being the dreaded judge is that we simply choose the easier route of blurting out the answer instead of supporting the other to solve the problem with empathy and love. It saves time! Humans are lazy! The short cut from A to B has always been more attractive and in many cases, it might save time and energy. However, when it comes to the need to think a little before we speak, we both know that a little thought before we discharge our response can make the difference between a solution or a kick-off.

There's also our knee-jerk, 'fight or flight' response in the heat of the moment, when anger takes centre stage and we instantly switch to using the 'downstairs brain,' as opposed to the rational part upstairs, it seems to us that the only thing that's going to make us feel better at that moment is to quite simply 'blow.' There is much evidence to prove that the act of shouting, screaming, slamming something down on a tabletop, or worse is a sure fire way of venting stress and anxiety. However, it fails to then address the inevitable fall-out afterwards of exactly what we needed to scream at, throw across the room, bruise, smash, shoot several holes in, or worse.

Peer pressure is another one that jumps oh so securely into the driving seat when we're with anyone who's got a axe to grind. All it takes to get the judgmental juices flowing is a little 'beef' one of us may have with some unsuspecting soul and that's it! The ease with which the rest of us get swept up in a conversation charged with back-biting is so tragic it's hilarious!! A close friend of mine who has been helping me proofread this book told me about a recent visit she made to a coffee shop with her older sister and her friend. She said that since reading these pages, she has started to see the world in rather a different light. She explained that from the moment she sat down with the other two ladies, she was instantly struck by the fact that at least 90% of their conversation consisted of straight ahead 'bitching.' First about each other's spouses, then each other's bosses or colleagues, then a sales assistant that one of them had been served by a week ago got it in the neck, then her sister's neighbour! The cull continued unabated until the two of them looked quite worn out. My friend said that she had been going for coffee with these two for many years, but now, it was like she was watching the scene through a different lens. She used the word 'shocked' to describe how she felt when she noticed how much the two ladies engagement with each other depended upon them meeting each other's responses with something equally judgmental to say, turn by turn. I mean, how else in a social 'catch-up' are two people going to make each other feel good and fulfilled without helping each other look down on others?!

The next reason for our propensity to choose a judgmental outburst dates back to infancy where, as soon as we were told not to do something, well, that was precisely what we wanted to do! 'Don't you dare say that to your sister!', 'If I hear you say that again, you're gonna be in for it!' Many of us believe it's old Lucifer, making it seem more perversely attractive to be judgmental, mean and hurtful in our response to someone else, the juicy, forbidden apple! Others see it very simply as 'flicking on the defiant switch' to anyone who warns us of the consequences if we 'dare to do it again.' It instantly becomes a dare, a challenge! Egos lock eyes and horns when little jack knows mum is waiting to see if he's got it in him to follow through and actually do what she told him he's not allowed to do. The key problem here is that we prefer to tell our kids (in a completely judgmental way) to stop doing something wrong instead of just focussing on telling them to do something right. As soon as we blurt out 'stop doing that right now!' all that child (or even adult!) is going to want to do is watch our face as he carries on and DOES that thing! To hell with what's right or wrong, she is not going to win! I am going to win! However, If we want Jack to stop throwing food at his sister across the dinner table, then we say 'Jack, I want you keep your food in your plate and eat it. Let's think for a moment about millions of other people around the world who don't have any food at all to eat. How lucky are we to have this food on our table?' It's called positive behaviour management, developed during the 80's and 90's that focusses on proposing the solution as opposed to dwelling on the problem.

I'm almost done with racking my brain for all the conceivable reasons why we decide to 'pee on someones chips' as my old store manager used to so eloquently put it. Its when we feel threatened. In the thick of battle, the hubby is with wifey at the kitchen table and wifey lets rip about how lazy he was yesterday to ignore the pile of laundry she left for him to put away. Hubby manages to take the defensive stand and retorts with 'I was too busy doing all the other things you ordered me to do!' He is about to relax and steer conversation towards less turbulent skies when he suddenly clocks her expression. It's an expression he has seen appear many a time just before another attack. He can't be certain but rather than take the chance, he opts for his own Pre-emptive attack in order to stop hers in it's tracks! 'Id like to ask you something now. As the person who always moans at us all for not putting our shoes in the cupboard, why are you regularly leaving your own shoes lying around?' Feeble at best but better than an empty barrel. Confrontations become petty primary school playground stand-offs that are all about nothing more than defeating the other by any means necessary. What we fail to factor in when wading in for the victory is the fall-out and more importantly, how easily we could have chosen different words to avoid the ugly end.

Finally, as common a reason as any of the above for choosing a judgmental response is that internal judge we all have inside us that keeps reminding us of our own circus marquee rammed from ground to the top with all our perceived short-comings, weaknesses, vulnerabilities, mistakes made, prejudices and traumas. All these 'flaws' that we see in ourselves, translate into us casting our judgmental floodlight on everyone else. A kind of a defence mechanism designed to compensate for what's going on inside.

The acknowledgment of these damming truths comes to us the moment we reflect on these factors that drive us down the smooth, slippery and oh-so lazy highway to Judgmentalism.

How does it feel when somebody speaks to us in a judgmental way?

Put simply, when spoken to like this, people of all ages will normally take offence and needless to say it's instant! They feel patronised and belittled. They feel that the person speaking to them is really saying they are better than them, cleverer than them and without their help, they would not have been able to solve the problem themselves. Although the 'judgmental culprit' usually has no intention of making their victim feel these emotions, they will still initially respond in this way. Why? Because they like most of us have been taught to flick our default judgmental switch to 'on' since birth. When I think back on my time as a child in Dudley, 5 older siblings in the house, mum, dad and whichever other relative was staying with us for whatever reason, I try to remember moments when family members were not being judgmental with each other. Moments when I couldn't hear someone having a pop at someone else and then the ensuing rabble, followed by the few days of awkward silences, until things just click back into place, ready for the next blow-out! I can't remember many at all.

The judgmental response is happening all day everyday everywhere and between people of all ages, regardless of the community they are from or the language they speak. The judgmental response is usually the first choice of response too as we seem to find it easier than the prospect of considering our response first. Most of us are also used to expecting others to be judgmental with us. It's a two-way response that is the universal trigger for just about 99.99% of all conflict in the world.

Here are a couple of examples that I'm sure would be familiar to anyone reading this:
A sister tells her brother that she felt very upset by the way he spoke to her that morning and she just needed to get it off her chest. Instead of looking concerned and even remotely apologetic or even asking her to explain it further, he simply raises his voice and retorts with 'well, you were rude to me last weekend when I left my socks in the living room, but I'm not throwing it in your face!

My work colleague told me recently that he loves cooking when he is alone in the kitchen. He feels totally at peace, focussed on the processes he is working through and taking his time. He can even multi-task, stirring the white sauce while peeling the potatoes, but as soon as his wife walks in, he's instantly seized by an involuntary and overwhelming feeling that she is watching him and judging his actions. She might have only walked in to empty the dishwasher or put the kettle on, but the mere fact that the principle house cook has entered the kitchen is enough to topple his confidence and trigger his paranoia that she is about to point out a key mistake in what he's doing.

One that left me quite shaken, not just from laughter but then actually believing that this guy probably could go to these lengths to get his judgmental fix was a stand-up comedian in India. He was going to lengths to explain how, since their wedding, he and his wife had gradually become more and more obsessed with pointing the finger at each other, to prove the other wrong, to catch each other out, then to stand on the podium over their partner with presiding height and watch them squirm, shrink in submission. All pretty normal behaviour between couples I hear you think, however the audience really fell about when he explained what usually happened when the family had a flight to catch. His wife would always suggest another route to the one he was taking in order to avoid traffic and get there on-time. Needless to say, she would also do this so that she could then spend the entire flight gloating about the fact that they only arrived on time because she insisted on another route to the airport. He explained that he would deliberately follow her suggestion and secretly pray that they would miss the flight just so that he could say 'well that was your bloody stupid idea for going another way wasn't it!' This guy actually preferred to waste all the flight ticket money just for the ultimate judgmental fix of watching his wife's face when he took gold on that 'I was right all along' podiums top tier. He even mentioned that the temptation to slow down a little when following 'her' route was always a little more than he could resist!

So, this ego driven need we have all been brain-washed into growing up to prioritise in our lives is the singular, most potent, yet covert and illusive force that keeps us down. Jumping to be judgmental actually holds us back, all day every day. It cripples our own self-confidence, self-respect and self-worth, as well as that of others around us, creating and maintaining the kinds of severely unhappy and dysfunctional environments that breed nothing but negative outcomes for all.

How does it feel when somebody speaks to us in a non-judgmental way?

Wow! When we're spoken to in a non-judgmental way, every part of ourselves feels good. As Nina Simone sings of the empathy even nature shows us in its connection with us 'birds flying high, you know how I feel, the sun in the sky, you know how I feel, breeze driftin on by, you know how I feel, it's a new dawn, it's a new day, it's a new life for me...and I'm feeling good...

You see, what happens to us when we all start to be non-judgmental is exactly what we need, mind, body and soul. Because there's no need for us to become defensive, switching to that 'fight or flight' state, we remain cool, calm and focussed on getting the most out of whatever situation we're in. whether that's solving a problem at work, cooking tonight's dinner or playing team sports, our emotional resilience goes up, our whole physiology is optimised, and we are at our best. It's in this state that we are most likely to show no-judgmentalism and empathy ourselves too. If we look specifically at partners, we see the power in nurturing friendship between them. Dr Gottman says, 'friendship fuels the flames of romance because it offers the best protection against feeling adversarial towards your spouse.' We all know that one of the foundations for maintaining a feeling of friendship is to control those all-pervasive impulses to be judgmental.

This flip side, when we look at the broader payoffs of walking the earth non-judgmentally, we do really start to see the light! We start to see that by learning the skill of not clashing with others, of not just looking for reasons to point the finger of doom at someone in order to make ourselves feel better, the positivity starts very quickly to seep into everything we do and experience. Our popularity skyrockets with everyone because we're simply not getting into scrapes. It also starts to seem like everywhere we turn, those around us are now poised at the starting block ready to help us out, regardless of how busy they are themselves.

Another very very beautiful effect of sticking to this 'non-judgmental you' is that whenever you make a mistake, be it at work or home, people will always be there to back you up, instead of dropping you in it. Now the reason why they will do this is the 'non-judgmental you.' They will have got to know the 'non-judgmental you' and they will go out of their way to bail you out because they believe that you would do exactly the same for them. In fact by the time you do need them to bail you out, the 'non-judgmental you' will have already bailed them out of a problem, which has already brought them closer to you, respecting you and trusting you. So, at this point the thought of them not running to your rescue is pretty much unthinkable for them.

Now, because right now in the world, most of us are dealing with each other judgmentally, that miniscule number of us that do manage to break through into more non-judgmental behaviour will then start to be seen as the go-to person, a problem solver, 'the fair one', the one that's not going to judge me, the one we can go to if we can't resolve our dispute ourselves, 'I know she'll keep it to herself', if there's anyone I can trust, it's her. Our whole profile in front of the world is altered. We are valued, and the effects of all this external profit on us and how we feel about ourselves is rather priceless. It is the stuff that makes super humans. It is the driving sustenance that nurtures in each of us the very best of health, happiness and prosperity.

In Dr John Gottman's book Raising an Emotionally Intelligent Child, he explains the findings of more than four decades of research his institute have carried out on observing how families engage with each other at times of high stress. He proves that children who are treated with non-judgmental empathy, love and patience will grow up with the following qualities:

- They are able to make and maintain more meaningful and long-term friendships
- They are better at calming themselves down after getting angry or over-excited
- Their brains and bodies are better developed inside and out
- They actually get ill less because their physiology that deals with their emotions is working at its best, so their immune systems are far stronger than those of children who are not being shown enough empathy and non-judgmental responses
- Their attainment levels in education are much higher

Inevitably they do much better in life than those children who have not had such emotionally stable and fruitful childhoods.

Dr Gottman's research comes together to give us the 5 steps of Emotion Coaching which are an extremely simple guide in how to speak with your child (and indeed each other) in a way that helps you not only connect with them but also teach them something, and the research shows that when we engage with our children like this constantly, our children start to develop the kinds of qualities listed above. The 5 steps go like this:

1. **To become aware of the other persons' emotions.**
   To simply notice that the other person is in need of support.
2. **To see their state as an opportunity for connecting to them and teaching.**
   To ask them what is bothering them and offering to listen.
3. **To help them find words to label their feelings.**
   When they start to share their experience with you, you simply help them to put words to how they might have felt. Gottman's research proves that when a child is in a stressful state, they find it very difficult to understand exactly how they're feeling, especially when they still don't possess enough emotional vocabulary. However as soon as we start to help them to label how they are feeling, they quickly become less confused about their feelings and this does two very powerful things:

A, they start to calm down because they suddenly have words to describe how they're feeling, and this has stimulated their Vagus nerve which we will explore in a lot more detail in the next chapter.

B, they suddenly feel like you are connecting with them, because you are giving them your precious time and attention. You are already showing them that you sincerely care about them, about what they are going through, about wanting to work with them to solve their problem. They start to trust you.

4. **To listen empathetically and validate their feelings.**
   To show them that you know how they are feeling and that you accept their feelings.
5. **To set limits on their behaviour whilst at the same time helping them to solve the problem.**
   To question them with the aim of getting them to acknowledge their own part in the situation and coming up with ideas of how to solve the problem without spelling out the solution to them.

Now, I hate to be blunt, ok, I don't as long as it's not tripe, but I feel it's completely necessary to say that from these scientific findings that spanned more than 40 years and many like it, we all need to shudder at a particular thought. It is, that so many of us have, despite having had fairly stable up-bringings, (we might even use the words happy, memorable or loving), even the most happy amongst us will still acknowledge that the kind of judgmental behaviour we have witnessed right the way through childhood, into adulthood and up to this moment, has left most of us way behind the super child described in the 7 points above.

My point, and this is one that I believe whole-heartedly, is that even the most functional of us in society, any society, would have delivered incalculably more positive outcomes in our lives if society had been far more focussed on tackling the scourge of judgmentalism.

It's a no brainer to reflect on how far from these 7 descriptors our children are who have to go through childhoods filled with trauma and abuse, but there has been and still is an enormous deficit of non-judgmental, empathetic and loving behaviour between parents and children, bosses and employees, teachers and pupils everywhere in the world today, and at every level of society.

In a later chapter, we will look at some of the real life, real time examples of such grotesque judgmentalism being displayed at the lowest echelons of society right up to the highest. Make no mistake, judgmental conduct pervades all cultures, languages, faiths and nationalities.

One thing I really grapple with that hits home the urgency of this book is when I reflect on the staggering innovations and advancements the human race has made and continues to make in all parts of our lives; from the Internet and modern day forms of travel to engineering wonders like the Palm Islands in Dubai or our research on outer space. We can do all of these things and more, yet as soon as someone speaks to us in a way that we don't like, we break apart. We switch. We forget that we ever had the capacity to hold back our emotions in order to avoid a confrontation and we simply 'vent!'

So, a pretty simple equation:

Most of us are judgmental all the time, therefore most of us are being judged all the time, this means all of our insecurities, paranoias and defensive knee-jerk behaviour surfaces and perhaps frequently blows out of the water and into the clouds when we 'flip our lid' at each other. Now just press repeat each morning for so many of us.

This issue, of the fact that we are, all of us, where ever we live in the world, wired up to first choose a judgmental response, then quite prepared to deal with the often inevitable confrontation that will follow, is what this book is setting out to explore. It remains an enigma. Right from our judgmental trail-blazer Lucifer, through to our children today, whether they are growing up semi-naked, bare-footed within a tribe in a remote jungle, or by a Hollywood starlet's super-nanny, I'd like to prove that when people start to embrace a more non-judgmental approach to their lives and interactions with their world, we will start to take the next critical step in our evolution. Until then, so many of us, our relationships and our own progress through life is, I struggle to find a better word, buggered.

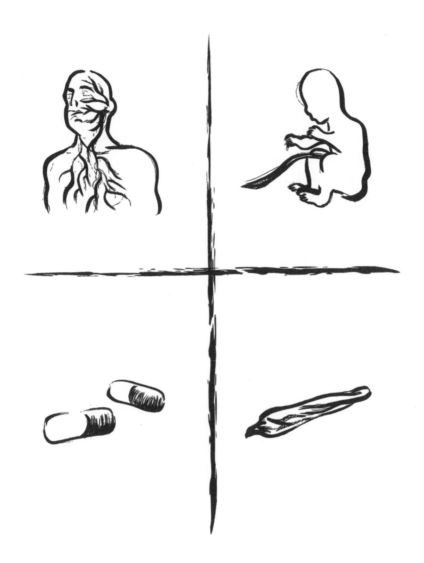

CHAPTER 2:

Sad Brain, Sad Body

Ok, so having explored what it is to be judgmental and some of the main reasons why we do it, I feel it's only logical too, to touch on some of the affects that our perpetually judgmental lives have on our health in general. And yes, I'm fully aware that this chapter sounds like another 'crier of all things grim' but I'm sorry folks! It's gotta be done! In the same way that, before studying behaviour and emotions, I only gurgled when asked what the word judgmental meant, I was also completely unaware of how instantly, directly and profoundly our emotions dictate the health of our bodies.

Now that we've established that it's judgmental responses that trigger our stresses, anxieties, aggressions, mood-swings and general desire to (for want of a more sensible description) knock someone's block off! I'd like to introduce you to a very very close friend of yours that, the chances are, you haven't met yet. In fact, this friend of yours is probably the most sincere, candid and innocent mate you'll ever have. She's even got a name! And her name is Vagus. Not the city in Nevada, but the pretty fat nerve that goes from your brain stem and meanders down to connect with and regulate a number of your major organs and functions like your heart, your lungs and your abdomen. Vagus provides you with movement functions for the muscles in your neck responsible for swallowing and your speech. She's also in-charge of your digestive tract, your respiration as well as your heart-rate functioning (the feminist in me opts for using 'her'). Vagus has also been known as your bodies 'communication superhighway' because she is your brain's main channel of conversation with the rest of you.

There are actually numerous other jobs that Vagus has been slogging away at in the background for you since you were a 24 week old foetus so, I think it's only right for you two to finally 'break the ice!' Vagus, you. You, Vagus. Wow! Just think, you're both the same age and you've been through some s**t together up to now, but I'm also duty bound to let you know something that Vagus would only appreciate me telling you. That is, that Vagus can only really do her job properly when you're feeling relaxed and happy. Yes, the dreaded caveat of your relationship with your newest and oldest friend is that whenever you are in an anxious, stressed and confrontational state, she stops doing her job properly, because your body's survival mode needs to take over. This is when your heart rate increases, the bronchial tubes in your lungs dilate to take in more oxygen, your muscles tense up, and more glycogen is turned to glucose – all to help your body run away from or fight things that threaten it. This is known as the 'fight or flight' state.

It's about now that we start to realise why, when we are constantly stressed, anxious, depressed, JUDGMENTAL with each other, that we can so often become ill. Through the Vagus nerve, our bodies respond in an instant! My horrible affliction when I'm stressed is a bad stomach or mouth ulcers. What's yours?

I saw this day in, day out during the 12 or so years I spent working as Teacher and Learning Mentor in PRUs around the West Midlands in some of the country's most deprived neighbourhoods. PRU stands for Pupil Referral Unit. These are mostly old 1960s/70's buildings located fairly discreetly in the back streets of almost every town and city in the country. Society's guilty secret. They are a metamorphosis of the old Borstals that were crosses between prisons and very badly equipped youth clubs for those kids whose behaviour was just too disruptive for mainstream schools. So, when a school decides that enough is enough, the child gets carted off to the nearest PRU where, unknown to them, they will invariably spend the rest of their schooling years there. Why? Because like any prison inmate that settles into the institutionalised life behind bars, these children suddenly find like-minded children in their new environment. Children who have already settled into the PRU way of life and are keen to take the new recruit under their wing, show them the ropes and watch them 'flourish.' In the more urban neighbourhoods, these PRU's are the best recruitment sources for all the local organised crime industry, like the 'County-lines' trade or for sexual exploitation.

There's a fundamental difference between the idea these children have of 'normal behaviour' and the idea that the vast majority of children have, and a simple way to explain this bizarre polarity in these kids' heads is a child in a mainstream school and a child in a PRU who are approached by a staff member and asked why they are disrupting the lesson.

The mainstream child will normally respond by stopping their disruptive behaviour, take the confrontation on the chin and probably not argue back. They will even expect and accept the sanction coming their way and still dread the phone call home.

The PRU child on the other hand will rarely give the same response, unless of-course he or she is doped up with ADHD medication designed to dumb them down for the day. For them, the classroom presents an audience made up of a few other PRU children with EBDs (Emotional Behavioural Difficulties), all expecting them to challenge the Teacher, be abusive, defiant, even aggressive. Anything it takes to defeat and humiliate the adult confronting them. Why? Because to respond to a challenge of any kind with defiance and a counterchallenge is seen as normal behaviour. Why? Because they have grown up in a domestic environment where everyone around them including their parents, have almost always behaved like that. Why? Because generally, their parents were excluded from mainstream school too. There is a very high number of these families, from the lowest socio-economic parts of our communities, for whom this pattern of negative outcomes and often involvement with the criminal justice system is inter-generational. They'd actually keel over if one of their kids wasn't excluded from school pretty early on. But make no mistake, many of these parents love their kids as much as any of us. They see the same negative trajectory their kids are on and more often than not, want their kids to change. They dread the thought of their kids following in their footsteps, but when I sit down with them and tell them how worrying their child's behaviour is and I watch the tears flow, they say only one thing. 'I don't know what to do to change him. I've tried everything. He just doesn't listen. So, what else can I do other than shout and scream?'

The mere thought that their child's misbehaviour might be down to something they're doing, something about their lifestyle or life choices is at first just plain silly!

Here are a few examples of real life chaos that I've encountered during the years I spent working with so many families of children excluded from school, that demonstrate the opposite end of the parental spectrum to our own idea of 'normal parenting.'

When Harry used to put a chair through a window in one of my lessons, or put his fist through a small door window, cutting up his hand (the small glass windows that contain a wire mesh) I used to call his dad to let him know. His predictable response was always 'well he's in a naughty school, isn't he?' what else do you expect him to do?! I went to a naughty school too!'

Another middle-aged single mother of around seven children (all working their ways through the PRU system) had uploaded a video onto her Facebook page of her fighting another mum in the local park. She can be seen first handing her hair extensions, mobile phone and small tin of marijuana to her boyfriend who then dutifully began to record the fight. It was quickly uploaded onto Facebook and staff sat that afternoon watching the video, trying to work out how to respond to her kids and the fall-out they would need to deal with the next day in school.

I remember it was exam time in July and the GCSE Science exam was about to start. I was looking intently out of the hall window waiting for a particular student to appear. He had serious behaviour issues especially when in school and was always stoned. He eventually arrived half an hour into the exam, with his dad and their dog. Right outside the school gates, father and son were burning down the rest of a joint together, hurriedly passing it to and fro and taking hasty deep puffs to finish it off, obviously because both were worried about getting him into the exam before it ended! Eventually, red-eyed and wreaking of the herb, he entered the exam hall and began fighting a losing battle with his memory and his munchies.

I visited the home, one morning, of a pupil whose attendance was causing serious concern with the school and who again, that day, hadn't arrived for her lessons. After knocking and waiting for someone to get out of bed and open the front door, her mum appeared, still half asleep but very welcoming. I was shown to the living room sofa while mum went to wake the daughter up, and after a few minutes both appeared and sat down on the sofa opposite me. The daughter lay down on the sofa, putting her legs over her mum's lap. Mum then proceeded to take a box of cigarettes from her gown pocket, take two out, pop one in her own mouth and then pop one in her daughter's mouth. Mum then took a lighter from the same pocket, lit her own and then her daughter's cigarette. Both began their morning ritual smoke as we began our conversation about the attendance issue. I remember her mum's opening words that set the tone for the rest of the argument with her daughter while I sat and simply watched. 'It's this f***ing idiot who won't get up in the morning!'

Needless to say, the permeant pandemic of judgmentalism across all communities and especially these groups, keeps these families down and keeps the kids in these constant states of 'fight or flight.' Now when these kids spend most of their childhoods in a state of fight or flight, their health, their brain development, their capacity to build and retain meaningful relationships and any future aspirations, all deteriorate. Statistics show, it's these kids that begin to self-harm or harm others. Its these kids that will eventually make up our future prison populations after committing a whole string of crimes against their community, their neighbourhood and their families and more importantly themselves. The government run Children's Commissioner reports that 100,000 kids are now being excluded or off-roll each year. Furthermore, the Commissioner also states that 85% of children in young offender institutions were from that cohort excluded from mainstream schools. A pretty loud alarm bell for all of us to start reflecting on how we can all, as communities start to tackle these issues together and creatively.

It's a chilling thought indeed when we reflect that people everywhere, right now, are so immersed in stress, depression and even thoughts of suicide, that the notion of ending it all actually becomes a kind of comforting companion. An option that will always be there for whenever they need it. The German philosopher Nietzsche once wrote 'The thought of suicide is a great consolation: by means of it one gets through many a troubled night.'

My take on all this is that through learning even a little more about what makes us tick, How our brains develop, how we can actively learn skills in controlling our emotions, we can truly start to command all of our lives and transform our futures.

However, there is an obstacle in our way that reaches to the high heavens. And that is the traditional expectation in most societies that once we're grown up, married, had kids and settled into a vocation somewhere, we don't need to learn any more. We know everything we need to know! Why because we're grownups now!! You know! First, we were kids and now we're adults! And now that we're adults, I'd like to see anyone tell me how to live my life!!!!! The notion of life-long learning is about as far away from most people in this world as my cat's food bowl is from the planet Neptune. Granted, for people who may live very remote and frugal lives away from any great metropolis, there might not be much need for parents to learn computer coding to help their kids pass their exams but even their detached world will consist of a similar ratio of people who want to continue seeking knowledge and who don't. The latter is normally the overwhelming majority, because a societal laziness, an inertia within most of us to gaining new knowledge because we are comfortable where we are and because we fear change is everywhere.

In the grand old hierarchy of numerous traditional cultures around the world, this thoroughly measured approach to what and how much youngsters should and indeed can learn is often not even seen as laziness, but what they learn is prescribed to them from A to Z. Any 'new knowledge' they might stumble upon is seen very much as frivolous and even potentially destructive to the established norm. Innovation and progress can just shoo!! Take a young girl in a traditional Pakistani household. My mum used to tell me that her childhood was exactly the same and sadly, it's still the same in many parts; from a very young age, the girls of the house were only permitted to attend school up to a certain age and level, as it's the boys who will need all the knowledge to become the bread-winners. Once that prescription was used up, they'd then be expected to stay at home to a, forget any academic knowledge they absorbed at school and college, and b, learn all the domestic work like cooking, cleaning and raising kids that they will need after their marriage, which will require them to go and live in their husband's home with his family.

I believe that this issue of limiting learning in our world today has its roots intertwined deeply with those of judgmentalism. It's simply when people, lacking the humility needed for the search of knowledge, assume they have already arrived. That they need not look any further, and from this conclusion springs forth all the judgmental arrogance and ignorance we see at the heart of all human conflict. This is also the very reason why my 'crusade' to get non-judgmentalism embraced by the whole planet is going to be a very long and arduous climb up a near vertical cliff face with no PPE.

CHAPTER 3:

What Does The Word
`Judgmental` Mean To You?

I'm gonna say this straight out of the starting gate – If I hadn't been working in Education and if I hadn't bothered looking into behaviour and emotions, I would probably give the same answer to the question above. I know this because the vast majority of people I have put this question to have always started their answer with that same abstract sound and out of the people who eventually did gurgle up an answer, many actually got it wrong. As soon as they hear the question, you see the eyes glaze over as all available power is channelled to the brain to find the answer! They 'buffer' for a few seconds while their microscopic neuro clerks sift frantically through connection files dating back to bell-bottom trousers. Until, of course, the clerks return with not the right answer, but a few possibles based on whatever they could glean from the question. This is normally based on clumping together the words 'judge' and 'mental' to see them as a kind of compound word. So, they deduce that it's definitely about judging and it's a no-brainer too that we're in the ballpark of the brain because of the word 'mental.' So many folks then declare that it must mean 'using your mind to work through a problem' or any other combination of words and descriptions that say more or less the same as that. who can shoot anyone for coming to this conclusion when generally, people seldom have the need to use the word judgmental in their daily lives?

In fact, I recently discovered the pretty disturbing fact that in my native languages of Punjabi and Urdu, there is no single commonly known word that would mean 'judgmental.' If you really insist on describing someone's behaviour as being judgmental in Urdu or Punjabi then you would need to go through the painstaking process of describing it, or you must resort to choosing a synonym for 'judgmental' like 'critical' which simply doesn't mean the same. The other, clearly more popular alternative is to get abusive! So surely folk could argue that if there is no word for it, then it doesn't exist! Judgmentalism is merely a figment of one's rather gaudy imagination.

This led me to wonder how many other languages were as guilty of this vocabularic neglect as my mother tongues were. Afterall, if the gate-keepers of a language have actually not even bothered to grant judgmentalism its own designated label, then perhaps that is a reflection of how little the people of that language are aware of the epic part that judgmentalism plays in keeping the flame of conflict alive in their communities. Or could it even be that they left the word out because where they live there is no judgmentalism? I think not.

So, I began to consult many of my friends and contacts around the world with this very question. However before delving into the multi-lingual issues encircling Lucifer's favourite word, I'd like to first share the following:

Here are a handful of answers I received from people I approached recently, here in England (the country where our vocabulary is already blessed with the dreaded word) and asked the question *'What does the word 'Judgmental' mean to you?'*

'Em, I think it's when you judge what's happening to someone else when they've shared their situation with you or their problem.'

'Em, I'm not sure exactly.'

'Er, well, it's just to judge isn't it, like making a judgement.'

'Em, when we're judgmental we look down on the other person. We might be insulting or offensive.'

'I think it means you're good at figuring out a problem and making the right judgment.'

'Ok, well, I think it means when you are the kind of person who's always making judgments about everything.'

Well, it's just to judge isn't it?

Em.

Er, well, I could judge you now. I could look at you or listen to you and just suss you out yeah!

I think it's talking about our ability to think about a problem definitely.

It's what a judge does but like, we do the same all day long.

Note. from all the people that I approached; the vast majority got the answer wrong so the verbatim answers above attempt to reflect that fact.

Now based on my belief that most of the public (including and especially me) are guilty of judgmentalism on a daily basis, it was no surprise at all that most got the answer wrong. This simply serves to further prove how miniscule the notion of judgmentalism and its pitfalls are in the mindset of most. Moreover, we've actually got a word in our vocabulary that means Judgmentalism and still people get stuck in answering questions about it! There is also little or no emphasis put on this word in our schools or workplace trainings either, where conveying the problem and solutions to judgmentalism could be done quickly and easily through simply giving practical examples of how a judgmental response can cause conflict as opposed to a non-judgmental response to the same scenario. However, there's a particular reason why workplace trainings still don't delve anywhere near deep enough into judgmentalism that we'll explore a little later in chapters six and seven.

So, getting back to my enquiries about the word Judgmentalism in other languages, I quickly began to get feedback from my friends and associates abroad, many of whom are Educators and Academics. Most of them told me in no uncertain terms that a, they had never been asked this question before, and b, they were surprised themselves to find that to their knowledge, there was no one well-known, single word in their native tongue that meant 'judgmentalism.' Just like the Urdu and Punjabi 'dead-end', they could only think of other words or phrases like 'critical' or 'too critical' to match with the word judgmental.

Below are a few examples of some of this feedback:

Punjabi – Ilzam lana – to accuse someone of something
Urdu – ghalat faisla - to make a bad decision
Hindi – kisi ko nicha dikhana – to belittle someone.
French – critique – 'critical.'
Dutch – Te kritisch – 'too critical.'
Spanish – Demasiado critica – 'too critical.'
Italian – Guidicante - Judgmental!
German – Wertend – Judgmental!
Pashtu –
Arabic – sarie alhukm – Judgmental!
Polish – osadzajacy – Judgmental!

Now surely common sense tells us that in order to start putting a thing right; to actively disseminate knowledge and guidance on how to solve a problem, people need to first be able to recognise and acknowledge that there is one, and if there is a problem then at least let's name it! When, in many languages, there isn't even a word that exactly means judgmental, the challenge of addressing it to eradicate it will inevitably be a tough one, particularly when the challenge we face is such a deeply ingrained, normal part of our everyday engagement with our world and with ourselves. What really highlights this absence of the word judgmental in so many languages is the universal acknowledgment by all I have spoken to, that yes indeed, judging others or anything too harshly is bad. They all agree on that, from the religious world to the non-religious, we're all, believe it or not, singing from the same hymn book. The first of these conversations happened with my cousins who were brought up in Pakistan but who now live here in England. Now as a fluent speaker of their native tongue, I already suspected that they'd struggle with finding a single word, and when that happened, It was the easiest thing in the world to then explain the meaning of the word judgmental to them. Why? Because the act of being judgmental is as familiar and natural to them as eating, breathing or sleeping. The momentary comfort in blurting out a judgmental response to anyone or anything pervades all nations.

CHAPTER 4:
A Global Language

So, we've established that in many different countries around our world, the word Judgmental figures fairly small in people's minds even though we all know that judgmental behaviour thrives everywhere and in all age groups. Again, this is clearly because we know, that as a human race, we have all adopted judgmentalism as our first and very normal response to each other. Despite the conscious knowledge that it makes all of our lives a lot more difficult every single day and in every conceivable way.

What I wanted to explore at this stage was how judgmentalism plays it's part in other cultures and even age groups in other parts of the world, and during the lockdown, the internet was again my window to reaching as many folk as possible. So, I spent many an hour surfing the great wide web looking for conversations, for people and for stories of judgmentalism.

Pakistan

It seems to make sense to start with my parent's homeland. You know, I was recently discussing this part of my cultural heritage with a friend. There is little more in my life that humbles me more than to reflect on how my parents simply 'upped and left' the land of their forefathers to come to England and start a new life. It's also clear to me and my siblings that a major driving force for them was to give their children a better chance to prosper in a more modern, progressive country than the one they had grown up in. This is the reason why, as I grow older, I feel an increasingly powerful responsibility to give back to my native homeland as well as the one I've grown up in. To use what little knowledge, skills and wisdom I have accumulated in my little brain and try to trigger some positive changes to a country still reeling, still finding itself, still in dire need of new ideas and good intentions.

This is why I recently delivered Emotion Coaching training via Zoom to all the staff of a school and college for orphan girls in Wazirabad, north Pakistan. This is a school that sprang up in the midst of a heavily industrial area, where most of these girls would have been funnelled into the local child labour market, had it not been for the Charities The Halimah Trust and Muslim Hands making this happen. The staff there are seriously committed to the school and college becoming an exemplar educational institution in a part of the world where one might least expect to find one.

Needless to say, the staff, just like most of us, were not clear on the meaning of the word judgmental, and again, because there's not a single word for it in Urdu or Punjabi, we needed to explain it's meaning through practical examples. However there was such humility in their willingness to listen to whatever I had to say and they spoke to me with the same respect and reverence that, in Pakistan, children are taught very strictly, to show a teacher.

A teacher in Pakistan and the wider sub-continent, is an object of almost holy status. To be seen as infallible, similar to the pedestal granted to a theological scholar or a medic. It was a truly humbling experience that left me actually struggling to clamber down from the pedestal they'd put me on. I kept reminding them that we were all educators in the world, but we were all life-long learners too. That during this training, there would and should be plenty for me to learn from them too.

I have encountered this extraordinary display of reverence before in Pakistani society which is beautiful in its recognition of those who are there to benefit communities both spiritually and physically. However, the dangers of seeing any human being as infallible and above question poses its own dangers, especially in a part of the world where a person can still get employment in a school without a criminal record check. Furthermore, I see this as yet another kind of judgmentalism turned on its head, where, instead of being over-critical, we're actually not critical enough. It's where people simply take your label, your identity, your credentials and perhaps the sound of your voice as a definitive marker of how much respect they ought to be showing you. The old 'judging a book by its cover' still lives on to delude us into both under and over estimating people.

Now getting back to how judgmentalism plays out in other cultures, it was fascinating to be delivering the training in both English and Urdu, with even a spattering of Punjabi. The reason for this is that I discovered just how innately judgmental the normal, everyday use of the Punjabi language is too, Just like English. What I had assumed from the start was that regardless of what language we speak or which part of the world we're from, our choice of vocabulary, intonation and overall body language is all conditioned to be judgmental. To use the technique of judgmentalism as a default switch for us, and again it points to the fact that it's just easier in the heat of the moment to spit out a judgmental response than it is to give it a little thought first.

It should also be pointed out that there are some key differences between Urdu and Punjabi, and in fact there are certain times/scenarios that require us to switch from one to the other. The key difference is that Urdu is like the 'queens English' of Pakistan. It's the official, formal and poetic language used in all the corridors of power, commerce and education. The national news is read in Urdu.

Punjabi on the other hand is more of a language of the street, of the working classes and by far, my favourite of the two. Why? Because even the most mundane sentence delivered in Punjabi, when delivered with exactly the right vocabulary, intonation and pitch will leave me and most who understand it, doubled over in stitches! There are copious amounts of humour in Punjabi. My wife may ask me, for example, why I've put so much salt in the curry, but it's the way she delivers that question in raw Punjabi that makes it so bloody funny!

But there's another reason why it's so funny. The humour is bursting at the seams with a massive helping of judgmentalism coated with a pretty thick layer of sarcasm! Now there's no debate about the fact that even contemplating the idea of trying to eliminate all judgmentalism from humour would leave humour in a pretty dark place. Humour lives and breathes off judgmentalism and sarcasm, and as a devoted proponent of humour and all the smiles, laughter, weak bladders and stimulated vagus nerves it brings with it, I'm actually faced with another reason why judgmentalism and sarcasm can be useful to us. God we're a complex bunch!

I believe the way to look at this is that when judgmentalism is simply used for the purpose of humour, then it's clearly ok. I'm a great believer that self-deprecation through humour actually helps us to develop greater humility. It's so important for us to be able to poke fun at ourselves because it's only when we can do this that we become more accepting of our perceived shortcomings.

On the other hand, if the intention is to upset someone then we're treading on perilous ground. Particularly when we think about the moment your partner asks you how they look in their new shoes and you're trying to decide whether to take revenge for last night's argument or not when you deliver your verdict! I'll say it again. We truly are a complex bunch!! It's pretty clear therefore that it's only when the world becomes a less judgmental one that people will be more emotionally equipped to meat out a good joke about someone else and more importantly take a roasting themselves!

So when I reflect on our use of judgmentalism in the Punjabi language, I can see that because it contains so much judgmentalism in its humour, this probably contributes to a lot more genuinely negative judgmentalism being flung around in homes as well as in the work place across the Punjab province along with my little home in black country Dudley in the 1970s!

There's even a suggestion here that wherever in the world we use more informal language to communicate with each other each day, there is perhaps more judgmental behaviour to be found there too. I make this assumption because when using more informal language, we also think and behave more informally too. This inevitably leads to less social constraints on what we discuss and how we discuss it. A perfect storm for a judgmental fix!?

America

A truly fascinating conversation was had with a father of two from Kansas, during one of my online strolls. As soon as I briefly explained the subject of my research, Geoff's whole demeanour changed in about 2 seconds from guarded scepticism to a 'well then why didn't you say that in the first place!' awakening to a subject he definitely had a thing or two to say about. It turns out that Geoff (not his real name) had a serious problem with being non-judgmental and he put a lot of this opinion down to a very conservative American view that if we can't judge then how can we challenge? If we can't challenge then how can we possibly progress, innovate, reform or move forward in any meaningful way at all?

This was simultaneously interesting and no surprise at all as I began to grasp his chain of thought. Geoff was explaining that so many of our young people today are being practically brainwashed in schools and universities into believing that they can and indeed should do whatever they want to do with their lives. Furthermore, for anyone to 'judge' them on those choices is somehow an infringement, a violation of their freedom to choose. He thought that was crap. He believes that making judgments, challenging others and not being afraid to do that is the very bedrock of how we make moral choices in all parts of our society. It is how we steer our young people away from anything we think is damaging for them, inappropriate or illegal.

My question to Geoff was this. 'Do you not think it's possible for a person to challenge or criticise someone without being judgmental?' I also felt it was important to clarify with him that to be judgmental is not to simply be critical but to be overly critical to the point that, instead of provoking thought and co-operation in the person we are criticising, we're instead offending them, upsetting them and ultimately provoking them to do the same to us. Hence the conflict. I followed this quickly by agreeing with my new friend whole-heartedly that as a race of people, so eclectic, so beautifully complex in our diversity in every way, we'd be fools to think that we shouldn't disagree with, challenge or criticise one another. The trick is *how* we do it.

Geoff was yet another of billions in our world; very well-intentioned folk who have had the very customary slant of 'disciplining through challenging' drummed into them all their lives. They believe that questioning and challenging comes with the inevitable territory of 'belittling, of intellectually dominating another to change their way of thinking. It's almost a necessary evil in the process of challenging someone. The inevitable collateral damage in the strive for moral justice.

I asked Geoff almost the same question as before, if he thought it was possible to challenge or criticise someone without making them feel any of those negative emotions. Could we do it using empathy, love and an open mind? I said 'open mind' because I said it's even possible that the 'criticiser' themselves may, ultimately realise they were the one who was wrong, in which case, they should already be armed with enough humility and courage to accept they were wrong.
Geoff agreed, but re-affirmed the whole point of this book when he said, 'but how many of us are prepared to do that...?'

Italy

The Italians are famous the world over for their emotions. Their legendary propensity for passionate expression whether in an argument or meeting a friend on the street, their association with all things emotional runs deep. In world P.D.A. rankings (public displays of affection) like holding hands, embracing or kissing, Italy is up there with Mexico and the rest of South America. Most of the languages of these places are based on Latin, also known as the 'romantic languages.' So, there is surely a safe assumption that Italians start to display this passion very early on in life.

This was more than adequately proven during another web surf for conversations on judgmentalism. I met Maria, a mum of 2 from Milan who began to tell me about her kids and how totally different their personalities are. Her 10-year-old girl Mia is a very passive character. She never complains and never even demands much. 6-year-old Emilio on the other hand is rather a different kettle of fish. Maria explained that right from when he was a toddler, Emilio needed little prompting to exhibit emotion, be it protesting when he didn't get what he wanted or victorious fists punching the air when he completed his building block tower on his bedroom floor.

However now, at the ripe old age of six, Emilio has already refined his emotional expression to 'Brandoesque' waves of the hands when tucking into mum's spaghetti meatballs or angry little 'alpha male' outbursts when Mia gets what he wants. Maria remarked that if Emilio could get hold of a gun at times like these, she dreads to think what he might do. This was promptly followed, to my great relief, by a laughing emoji. So, I asked the question. 'would you say Italians are more judgmental than people from other parts of the world?' For around one and a half minutes the message feed went silent and I began to think that perhaps I'd said the wrong thing. She then typed 'I would be lying if I said no because amid all this passionate expression people are always judgmental. She reckons that if judgmentalism was wiped out from Italian society, there wouldn't be much of a society left. I then asked a similar question to the one I asked Geoff from America about if she thought people could express themselves in their Italian way without being judgmental. Maria said she believed they certainly could, but again, like our American friend, she told me I'd have a job on my hands!

My cyber journey throughout the judgmental world could so so easily have constituted a whole separate book. Perhaps, in the near future this may come to fruition. It would be about the only excuse I could devise to justify vanishing (for work purposes of course) for half a year to hang out in as many colourful, obscure and far-reaching ends of the earth. Gathering more stories and perspectives on the big J word.

However, for this book and this chapter, I feel we've established the existence of a pattern, a consistent supposition that:

A, we all need to see Judgmentalism 'in the dock' because it truly is the root of most conflict, regardless of where we live.

B, Judgmentalism has interlaced itself culturally with the fabric of just about every society on the planet

C, it seems clear that through conversation and debate, people everywhere can see this truth and more importantly, can start to think creatively about how to deal with it.

CHAPTER 5:
The Faith Take On Judgmentalism

Like much of this book, I'm venturing forth into this chapter with lots of preconceptions collected gradually and inevitably through my life. The primary preconception I have for what I'll discover here is that all religions will condemn negative judgmentalism. From Satanists and Druids to Jews and Sikhs, I'm more than certain that a blanket damning of judgmentalism will prevail.

However I'm also already convinced that there will be a question I will ask many of these people of various faiths, that most, if not all will find difficult to answer, and that question is 'Why are religious people amongst the most judgmental in the world?'

Islam

Now, as ancient as the chicken and egg, my brother recently told me that from the perspective of Islam, one of the first sins ever committed was, yes, no prizes for guessing, an act of judgmentalism. It's when Satan, also one of God's creations, was asked to prostrate to, and acknowledge the greatness of Adam, God's first created man, shaped and given life from the clay of the earth. It's at this point that Satan turned, deciding that God's new creation wasn't worthy of such merit, and vowed from then on, to lead man astray towards a life of sin. So, the devil himself carries the accolade for the first ever recorded Judgmental response. A pretty grim flag bearer for the cause of judgmentalism without a doubt.

Christianity

The Christians have a slightly different take on how Satan found his niche in history, believing that he simply fell from Grace and then tempted Adam and Eve to eat from the forbidden fruit. A crime for which they were banished to earth and where Satan, then, would devote himself to leading them astray. All unadulterated acts of judgmentalism of course, and the Bible itself makes very clear reference to seeing judgmentalism as one of the great sins of the church.

'Because judgment without mercy will be shown to anyone who has not been merciful.' James 2:13 or 'Do not judge or you too will be judged.' (Mathew 7:1)

Sikhism

This faith is also clearly mobilised against any notion of judgmentalism. In fact, in Sanskrit, one of the principle and most ancient languages of Sikhism, there is apparently no word for renunciation of others because to commit such an act is to be furthest from the prospect of enlightenment. (the highest spiritual level that can be attained by a person).

Hinduism

The Hindu Faith is equally as robust in its disapprobation of all things judgmental. In Hindu scripture we are warned about being harsh and Judgmental of other's faults, even when we can clearly see them. This is because we're advised to focus on our own faults first. I can see the wisdom in this approach where, if we all individually focus on transforming our own behaviour rather than that of others then the temptation to be judgmental vanishes.

'The vile are very prone to detect the faults of others, though they be as small as mustard seeds, and persistently shut their eyes against their own, though they be as large as Vilva fruit.' Garuda Purana 112

Judaism

'Do not judge thy comrade until thou hast stood in his place.'
Mishnah, Abot 2.5

The Jewish faith uses analogies to convey how abhorrent it is to be judgmental. The faith teaches that to unfairly damage someone's reputation is akin to murder, and to take a life is like destroying the world. So, slander is an unthinkably serious sin as clearly there is nothing worse than destroying the world. However, Rabbi Barry silver, in an article for Sun Sentinel, quotes from Jewish scriptures when he says, 'rebuke the wrong-doer, lest you share in his iniquity.' Commands like these seem to contradict each other, until we are told that we must be extremely cautious when uttering harsh judgments against others. It's clearly about getting one's facts straight before speaking up, and when we do, then it needs to be as measured as possible and done with the right intentions.

Now, it's plain to see that all of the key faiths are mobilised together in their stance against judgmentalism, and the main reason for this is that it's pretty much a 'no-brainer.' To be judgmental is considered by the faithful to be sinful. Period. It is universally seen as the opposite to being patient, humble and empathetic. However, this is precisely why my controversial question, asked at the start of this chapter, needs desperately to be explored. 'Why are religious people amongst the most judgmental in the world?'

When surely it's the religious folk in our world that are supposed to be the walking talking, living breathing examples of the faith that they represent, why do so many of us from all different faiths feel more judged, compartmentalised, and dictated to by our spiritual leaders than attracted to them and the religion that they want us to embrace alongside them?

It seems to me to be the ultimate contradiction, or, at the very least, the risk of one, where a person (not a divine messenger) who willingly assumes a position of spiritual authority over others is expected, with that elevation, to become infallible and above question. I'm trying, I believe, in vain to imagine this person; he or she (usually he) will have struck the perfect and seemingly impossible equilibrium between complete non-judgmentalism and leading others spiritually. In my life, I believe I have yet to meet such a human being. Someone who is never judgmental in their responses to those that they lead! Wow! The holy grail! The golden fleece! The sanctum of worldly spiritual leadership. However, the reality is rather different, bringing us back down to planet earth with a heavy, dull thud.

The reality is this. Most of us take little or no notice of how our faith, which ever one that may be, really wants us to behave with one another. It is the judgmental world that keeps us all from really, truly experiencing the beauty and harmony that can be found in our faith.

You want proof? Take a glance at history, filled to overflowing with wars waged on religious supremacy and hate. For so many of our so-called religious leaders, the corruption, abuse and hunger for wealth and dominating power over the masses leaves little room for polishing up on their own non-judgmental skills, let alone preaching them to their followers. In reality, they often preach the exact opposite, declaring to their own 'flock' that they are the truly faithful and the others are not. The hypocrisy of which makes anyone's skin crawl.

In fact, I believe that the darkest and most egregious acts of evil in this world today are committed in the name of religion. Like the widespread scourge of sexual/physical abuse of children in many religious institutions across the world, or the phenomenon of Satanic ritual torture, rape and murder of children. A practice that right now, is on the rise across the world.

No folks, if we're looking to our religious leaders for guidance in how to be better human beings to each other, then, in many cases (not all) we are on to a loser. You see, again, this harks back to what we discussed in chapter 1 about greater power bringing greater responsibility. about the fact that although we may clamber to positions of power, influence and respect in our lives, the 'ego massage' of a judgmental response or feeling and even wanting to feel like we're in some way shape or form superior to someone else is something that we have all become hard-wired to crave, whether we're in a Gurdwara, Mosque, Synagogue, church or Mandir.

Another real and deeply damaging symptom of people's misinterpretation of religious teachings is the danger in religious zeal, especially when it's newly found, that can actually nurture more potent feelings of judgmentalism, arrogance and superiority in the hearts and minds of the more vulnerable amongst us than in someone who has always practiced their faith in a certain consistent way. Those of us who have experienced trauma in our lives, or had a sense of failure, suddenly have a power over others with this new knowledge and 'spiritual insight.' A stick to bash over the heads of our friends and more destructively, our loved ones who, until now were bashing us over the head for one reason or another! The tables have turned.

Our appearance and lifestyle will often change rapidly too, prompting us to impose new demands on those we live with. This is a power we've never had before, and it feels good. Why? Because all of a sudden, our family members, our friends and neighbours are looking at us differently. We choose, in our judgmentally spiritual stupor, to see it as more respect and reverence they feel for us than an awkward loss for words. This feeds that internal (and very secret) sense of 'special superiority' we're developing over others, without, of course spelling this out to anyone, especially not to ourselves! Until, of course, we are challenged and when this happens, the reality of our mindset comes pouring out. We will simply proclaim very sympathetically that the reason why the other person can't agree with us is because we are on a higher spiritual level to theirs. They are obviously not as close to God as we are! I kid you not! I have had first-hand experience of this level of delusional judgmentalism in not one but many many individuals I have come into contact with who, through some damned epiphany, have discovered their faith, read a few prescribed books, attended some events and then haven't stopped until they were about to lose everything.

You see them a year or so later and they're a broken, yet far humbler version of themselves before 'the great epiphany.' Needless to say, this is the stuff of extremism, and all it takes for devious minds to find such victims is to just look for vulnerabilities. Individuals who feel lost, who feel like there is something missing from their lives, loners who no one will miss are the choicest targets for these groups.

Now, as a believer myself, I'm extremely mindful of the thoughts and comments I've put forward here. I'm under no illusion that there are countless representatives of all the key faiths who are, by all accounts, good people with good intentions. However, this is precisely why I feel compelled to highlight these issues that exist everywhere in our faith communities. Issues that urgently need addressing by the gatekeepers of those faiths.

Faith and its essence, according to all of the religions explored above, involves a complete release from judgmental behaviour, and this is done by first accepting that we ourselves are fallible. It's only then, when we acknowledge this truth, that we can be prepared to subscribe to the notion of life-long learning. To the responsibility we all have to learn in order to progress, and to progress with the intention of empowering not overpowering ourselves and others.

CHAPTER 6:

Lead By Example?
Then We're All Screwed

One pretty safe assumption I have always had about why leaders of organisations great or small, would find the prospect of teaching non-judgmentalism to their people rather difficult, is very simply because they themselves are often the single most judgmental people in their organisation.

Many of them will have reached their zenith through the same process of carefully judged friendships, workplace scandals and 'favours for favours' that are such an utterly normal part of how so many of us forge our futures.

In fact, if asked, the majority of them will claim that it's perfectly natural and quite necessary for a leader of any level to use judgmental language to control and get the best out of their workforce (assuming of course that they even know the meaning of the word judgmental, which I'm already discovering most of them don't). Furthermore, they wouldn't have it any other way! I mean, imagine a workplace where the use of all judgmental behaviour was prohibited in the organisation's code of conduct! World leaders, Politicians, CEO's of multinational corporations, Movie stars, Movie Producers, Rock Stars, Super models, Royal family members, building site 'Gaffers' call centre Supervisors and corner store owners would be screwed. we would probably need more court houses built than residential ones just to cope with the liability caseloads pouring in by the second.

I and most probably anyone reading these words can testify from our own experience that we too have, numerous times in our lives, become embroiled in the kind of political deceit and social brainwashing that we're talking about here. Where leaders actually train their staff to 'crack the whip', to come down hard on the weaker elements in the organisation and set an example to the rest. To BE THE HARD-NOSED SARGEANT WHO GETS S**T DONE AND WHO NOBODY WOULD LIKE TO SCREW WITH for a couple of reasons:

> A. They will 100% have their cards marked if they speak up, so it's just a matter of time before they are accused of something, demonised, bullied, then forced to move on.

B. They fear that their reputation as 'a trouble-maker' will cling to them when they do eventually move on, thereby sabotaging their own chances of making that 'clean start' in their next position.

Judgmentalism is so clearly visible in that golden rule of progressing through the ranks by making the right friends and dumping on the people you need to in order to make it to the next step of the pyramid. Humans have done this since only God knows when, where people even organise their social lives outside of work hours to forge the right friendships based completely upon where they're trying to get to in their career. To hell with genuinely liking someone! What better reason is there to like them than the hope that they'll put in a good word for us at the next meeting, and when we do make the promotion, well, that's when we can really tell them what we think of them!! Serves them right!!!

We switch allegiances at work like kids in a nursery playground, nakedly and brazenly following the scent of power in order to make life easier for number 1. In fact even as adults, we attack and counter attack in workplace staffrooms exactly like a couple of 6 or 7 year olds. we haven't moved on from childhood. Only our appearance, our mushrooming hunger for material wealth and our vocabulary has grown. We are still those insecure, defensive, and self-absorbed beings that we were decades before.

One that has, in recent times turned my stomach to the extent that I had to leave the organisation, is seeing folk not only staying quiet after witnessing the malpractice of one of their leaders, but then actually backing up the culprit for one main reason. That is that the culprit will then remember that 'special favour' and in-turn, turn a blind eye when the other person decides to do the same. A toxic scenario of loyalty based only on fear of what the other could do to harm us. What a depressing, and real picture of our industrial world today. And all this goes on within our sparkling, progressive and innovative workplace legislation trumpeted by the leaders of our countries, where our unions too are left with hands tied, redundant when faced with our judgmental world.

Judgmentalism in the workplace also works wonders for dismantling the smooth running of any organisation. Especially the larger ones. The late Jack Welch, former CEO of General Electric in the US from 1981 to 2001, wrote a remarkable book after he retired called 'Winning'. The contents of which have, despite my complete failure to have won in so many areas of my own life, stayed with me. Especially the parts where Jack talks about the need for much greater candour between all the people in an organisation. From the CEO, right down to the cleaners. He writes 'let me tell you about the biggest dirty little secret in business, that's in every culture, every country, every society and every social class, there's this lack of candour.'

He's referring, of course, to the fact that the bigger the organisation gets, the less prepared the people at the bottom are to approach the people at the top. Those at the bottom find those at the top pretty much completely unapproachable; primarily because those at the top actually believe that they're in some way shape or form superior, more important, smarter and simply more fortunate that those beneath. Now whether those at the top actually mean to give off those vibes to their subordinates or not, both parties expect these hierarchical laws to be present even before they join the organisation. Why? Because society and especially our 'developed' world dictates this. Our class-ridden planet is governed entirely upon a judgmental pyramid of individuals, many of whom will be spending the majority of their waking moments devising ways to clamber to the dizzy heights of superiority without actually learning much at all about the communication skills they will need when they get there.

Even those that don't buy into this worldly delusion must accept that unless they're prepared to actively connect with their staff and nurture more candid and meaningful, more humane and democratic relationships with them, they'll just have to tow the line and:

• Accept their place in the pyramid of power.

• Accept that they will only have relationships (albeit plastic ones based on mutual interest) with those who sit alongside them in the pyramid

• Accept that when something in their organisation is going badly wrong on the ground that they can't see from their ivory tower, their staff on the ground will be too nervous about the prospect of flagging it up to them for fear of a finger being pointed at them. For fear of getting caught up in the all too illegal, immoral, yet completely common practice of back-stabbing within most of the organisations of this world.

• Accept, therefore that the little something that was going wrong on the ground will go un-checked and eventually snowball into something a s**t-load larger than a snowball. This giant, mutant snowball will then defy gravity, roll up the pyramid, gathering speed, consuming others on its way, until it finally arrives, smashing down onto the leader's desk, too big to ignore and to resolve without that leader's head rolling down the pyramid like an Aztec sacrifice to the gods.

Eric Dodson, an American Psychologist, along with The Humanistic Psychologist Carl Rogers both help to explain why, as a human race, particularly in the so called 'developed' world, we generally resort to judgmentalism all day, every day. They believe that the modern, technologically, beaurocratically and industrially advanced world encourages us to treat each other like objects most of the time, to manipulate, judge and use each other so often and so relentlessly that when, on the rare occasion any of us do actually try to connect with each other in any more meaningful way, it can feel almost inappropriate, unexpected and even insincere! We're as institutionalised in the prison of judgmentalism as an inmate doing life, but I completely believe people can change; I can change; you can change. No judgments of course...

CHAPTER 7:

I Don't Need You To Tell Me How To Manage My Staff!

There's an analogy that I regularly use in discussions when trying to explain how enormous I think the responsibility is on a countries government to guide its people. I see the leaders of a country in the same way that I see the parents of a family. In both scenarios, when those in-charge fail to lead in a meaningful, creative and loving way, then those being led will invariably go astray. If they don't go astray then it is nothing short of a miracle. So when I reflect on how simple it is to become a 'boss', 'manager' or 'supervisor' in the world today, responsible for the sustenance and welfare of others, both emotionally and physically, I shudder at the reality that there is still an alarming gap in our provision to our people. There are still no legislative frameworks of mandatory training that people need to go through first before being allowed to lead others. The courses that do exist, don't even scratch the surface of tackling judgmental behaviour in the work place because, as discussed earlier, the vast majority of leaders in the world rely almost entirely upon judgmental communication to get results, and in many situations they do get the results. Just not any genuine respect or loyalty from their workforces. So whether it's in a street corner convenience store or the Amazons of this world, we all know the scandalous lack of people skills in so many of those that assume positions of authority in both public sector and private sector organisations everywhere.

Just my own examples alone that I have seen in my working life, of people in positions of authority, who have utterly failed to BE THAT LEADER, could fill the rest of the pages of this book and start to seep out over the covers and upside down into the margins! There would end up being scraps of paper covered in them too stuffed into the back! However, like in many other parts of this book, I'm really enjoying the research part, of asking as many people as possible for their thoughts and anecdotes. Of painting as broad a picture as possible of the issues themselves as well as people's thoughts about them.

So below is a spattering of real-life examples sent to me by many different people from various corners of the globe. No real names mentioned of course!

'I was in the staffroom and one of my colleagues, Geoff, very politely asked our department manager Simon why it was that certain staff were being allowed to leave early from another department, but not his. Simon simply but 'cuttingly' replied 'because THEY'RE working hard at the moment!' However, everyone knew that Simon's girlfriend was in that department, so there was little that they felt they could say.

'I was serving customers at the till. I'd had a pretty bad argument with a family member that morning and it was really playing on my mind. A customer approached and asked me a question. I was miles away and didn't realise. The customer repeated the question and I, still lost in thought, replied with a 'huh?' The customer looked a little put off and at that moment, the shop owner appeared and in front of the customer said, 'you've obviously got no idea how to speak to customers have you!'

'I was late recently for work. I'm normally always early and that allows me to get more of the early workload out of the way quicker. My line-manager came up to me and started to speak quite rudely to me about being late. I reminded her about the fact that I'm normally always early, to which she replied 'well, nobody asks you to come early do they! That's your choice!'

'One of my colleagues left our school recently and went to teach somewhere else. But she got into trouble there because of her conduct. I used to work with her when she was at this school and I used to always witness her being really harsh and accusational with the pupils. Once I even made a complaint about her, but nothing was done. Anyway, she has actually returned to this school even though she was being investigated for misconduct in the other school. We just know that it's because she is close friends with our head teacher. And there are so many other very qualified teachers who could do a great job for a much lower salary than she gets.'

'My boss is always quite serious, but occasionally he calls me a couch potato and tries to say it jokingly. Now, I'm quite a large lady and I'm a bit sensitive about my appearance at the best of times, so when he says that, I know damn well he's having a dig at me and trying to get away with sugar coating it as humour! It just comes across as really phoney.'

'We had a staff meeting where several issues needed to be discussed and our manager Lorna was present. As we started to go through each point and try to come up with an action plan for each, one member of staff very professionally and politely questioned Lorna's decision. Lorna's reaction was to immediately become defensive and quite confrontational. All this did was to visibly upset the member of staff asking the question who then continued to challenge Lorna. The confrontation escalated until voices were being raised and accusations exchanged had little to do with the original point! It was just really embarrassing to watch for everyone.'

Now, there is no doubt in the world that there are emotionally intelligent and genuinely good managers everywhere, but (I say this directly to them) you are a minority! Believe me guys! And that's why this stuff has to be shared and addressed.

I'd also like to talk about Peter Parker's uncle Ben who so so rightly declares that 'with great power comes great responsibility.' (Peter Parker – Spiderman) Never ever was a truer word spoken! Yet what little regard so many of our worlds 'leaders' give to the meaning and weight of these words. Why? Because they're not made to reflect on it. Remember the reasons we discussed in chapter one, about why we jump to being judgmental. It feels good (in that moment), it is easier than thinking a little more creatively about how to help someone solve a problem. It's the lazy leader's road to a little ego massage throughout their high powered and exceedingly stressful day. So surely, you exclaim, the buck stops with the people at the top! The company Directors and CEOs! Well, yes, it certainly ought to, however as mentioned at the start of chapter three, it's the leaders at the top who are so often the guiltiest of being old Lucifer's torchbearers of judgmentalism!

Personally, I find it outrageous that the very people who are responsible for others, (and in some cases tens of thousands of employees across the world) are under the government given delusion, that they can get away with talking down to others. Resting assured mind you, that those others will only ever consider talking back in the same way when they're on their way out of the organisation.

I say, 'government given' because it's government who are, just like 'mum and dad', failing to set the boundaries and prescribe these codes of conduct to the rest of us, because let's face it, so many of us only really toe the line when we absolutely have to. When it threatens to hit us in our pocket mainly. This rule applies to every single one of us. Just look at the issues of speeding on the road, claiming as many benefits as possible or paying out as little tax as possible. Therefore, the buck stops not with the Directors and CEOs but those that rule them. The parents of the nation 'so to speak.' It's not until government wake up to the sheer extent of judgmentalism's power to dismantle relationships, people's self-esteem and self-worth; it's not until government wake up to the fact that their own entire system of governance is based on a perpetual tennis match of accusations and counter accusations, most of which are lies designed simply to discredit and 'psych out' an opponent, this will never change. Just watch Parliament's Question Time on a Wednesday for 20 seconds and you will understand what a critical role judgmentalism plays in how these politicians survive and slay! Most of the dialogue consists of personal character assassinations. Probably not much different from the sound-bytes many of them flung around their Eton playgrounds as children, only now they command eye-wateringly high salaries to do exactly the same in a Saville Row suit. Oh, there I go again, stooping to the same level!!

In fact, even as I write this, there is a scandal involving none other than the government's Home Secretary over allegations that she bullied, victimised and forced the Home Office's most senior civil servant to resign from his job. He is now taking the government to court over his ordeal, and there has now been a full investigation over her behaviour. Needless to say that the government are not releasing its details. So, when those at the highest levels of society resort first to giving judgmental responses to others, what chance do the rest of us have?

What we need, at the risk of awakening the 'civil liberty' Troll from his exceedingly light sleep, is for government to pass some meaningful legislation about what people need to do if they want to be in-charge of others. A well-tailored CV showing a semi fictional track record of successful leadership should never again be sufficient. Sound like the seedlings of a dictatorship? Perhaps, until we start to reflect on how such legislation could transform and upskill not only how leaders lead, but at the same time, how the emotional and physical well-being of our workforces would flourish. Staff retention would sky-rocket, job satisfaction for employers and employees alike would thrive. As a result, output would increase, along with relationships both in work and at home.

Time Place Audience!

The other particularly bizarre aspect of judgmental behaviour at work compared to at home is that so many of us seem to have an almost completely separate persona that plays out for each of those places. It usually involves, unlike our Home Secretary just mentioned, most of us being very much 'on our best behaviours' at work, until we get home where, with our immediate family members, our inhibitions are left outside the front door to rot and we enter our 'complete comfort zone'. And it's in our 'complete comfort zone' that we allow ourselves and our judgmental behaviour to sprout wings and cavort wherever the hell it would like.

This has always baffled me! With strangers, so many of us are the picture of charisma, patience and etiquette. We are so quick to disguise ourselves with qualities reserved only for the outside world, for to even try to display them at home with immediate family would, frankly, look and feel downright fallacious. We'd get funny looks from our loved ones. Looks that would say 'are you feeling ok?' or 'that was a little awkward,' or 'oh I see, I wonder what you want now!' it simply would not wash. Why? Because everyone at home is completely used to seeing and dealing with the 'off-duty' version of us. When there's nobody to tell us that we have to behave in a certain way, we know we can get away with being complacent in how we treat each other. Although we know it's wrong, we still do it!

It's that scene I'll never forget where a mother, unaware that I was sitting on the other side of a partition was reprimanding her little boy in an empty waiting room. I could hear his clothes being grabbed and him getting shoved into a seat. She was practically growling at him! 'just you wait till we get home!' In an instant, the waiting room door opened and another person appeared, sitting down across the room, and Just as suddenly, the mother's tone, and I'm certain body language, even her facial expressions will have switched, becoming softer, more cajoling, even a little 'jokey' in front of the new 'outsider.' Clearly the last thing the mother wanted was to be seen by the stranger as a 'bit of a bully.' The last thing she wanted was for anyone to get a glimpse of the behaviour management strategies she uses at home! In short, the vast majority of us are like this! Admit it or not. So many of us maintain a similar Jekyll and Hyde double role of behaviour at home that we wouldn't dream of displaying at work. Hence the cases of domestic abuse increasing exponentially during the dreaded lockdown everywhere.

A married couple that I knew in recent years ended up separating because of the husband's abysmally bad temper at home. Their three kids and the wife had just about had enough of his outbursts after more than a decade of coercion, bullying and lying about finances, as well as having a child with another woman in another city! The mother finally decided to kick him out after threatening him with police involvement. Now, the interesting part is that he was a Director for a highly reputable organisation. His reputation for professional conduct, managing a team effectively, 'getting the best of people' and generally excelling in his role was known across the industry. Again, nobody in his workplace was privy to the character he played at home with his family, away from prying eyes and ears. Home for him was a different place with different rules, even though those at home were, just like those in his workplace, people with emotions, vulnerabilities, rights and boundaries. The thing that always struck me about their situation though was that his family had something that his work colleagues didn't have; a kindred attachment to him, that made his mistreatment of them all the more perverse. Unacceptable. Surely the relationships most dear and sacred to us are those we share with our families, our loved ones in our own homes. Therefore surely, if we are going to differentiate so starkly between work and home it ought to be home where we focus more on nurturing the best relationships than anywhere else in our lives. Although the ideal scenario is, of course, where we are consistent in how we engage with everyone at home and at work, surely our more intimate relationships are the ones that either make or break our emotional health far more significantly than our work relationships.

The story of separation above is an example of how the vast majority of us commit such destructive differentiation with each other at home. I believe it is partly down to simply familiarity and hierarchies in families. When we are growing up together, seeing each other daily and not being taught the kind of communication skills we all need to imbue each other with love and power instead of conflict, then the Jekyll and Hyde effect emerges. The older members of a family grow up to primarily learn how to win arguments rather than settle disagreements. To lord their authority over the minors rather than teach them about the grave responsibility that comes with being in charge, but how can they teach when they themselves have never been taught? This is what breeds disrespect, disregard and ultimately disappointment between human beings everywhere.

So imagine for a moment the prospect of approaching and engaging with our own family members at home with the same respect and regard as we do with work colleagues. Imagine, if just like at work, we were super sensitive to the feelings and needs of those we spend our time with. Working hard to show all the empathy, the comradery and protocol we know we HAVE TO show at work if we are to make it any further up the ladder. The noise in homes everywhere would not decrease but it would change from sounds of conflict to laughter and even more laughter. We would have finally got our priorities the right way round, and what does it take to make this shift? Firstly, an acknowledgement that it's our relationships at home with our 'own' that are worth not just fixing but nurturing; investing in with our time, our patience and our hunger for knowledge in learning these skills of connecting with each other. It truly is all about us mustering up that sacred humility we all need to take on new ideas that may challenge or even contradict our established wisdom.

From my own experience, my journey to this point in my life has been a long one, fraught with my own contradictions and hypocrisies. I struggled a great deal with curbing my own 'comfort zone' responses to my wife and kids that were so inconsistent and in fact totally the opposite of what I was learning through my work and research with children and families. It was so very easy to talk the talk of greater emotional self-regulation and thinking of alternatives to judgmental responses, but to then reign myself in during these moments of high emotion when all you want to do is VENT, was quite another story…

This is what it took:

Mistakes!

Elbert Hubbard once said, 'the greatest mistake a man can ever make is to be afraid of making one.' So, I made them! Constant mistakes. Relentless screw-ups mainly when I got upset or angry and would, just like the rest of us, flick the judgmental switch to ON. However as soon as I did and had delivered my first or second accusational or offensive remark to the wife or one of my kids, I'd stop right there, mid-sentence. Now to the on-looker this probably came across as looking like someone had accidently pressed the pause button, or I just started buffering! What it was, was simply me trying pretty desperately to catch myself in the act and stop myself each and every time I became judgmental. Eventually and inevitably, my judgmental responses decreased and so did my stress levels, because frankly, I wasn't pissing people off as much as usual!

Perseverance and commitment

It was certainly the mistakes, the constant and repetitive lapses into being so naturally judgmental that threatened to wear me down and throw the towel in very early on. What we've got to realise here is that what I was proposing to myself was a seemingly impossible challenge. I and all those around me had spent our entire lives engaging with each other in a certain way. I was entertaining the idea that I could change that, reprogram it, re-wire my brain, un-learn and then start afresh. The only force that kept me going was the knowledge that it was indeed our long long conditioned instinct to be judgmental to each other that gave food to all the conflict in the world yesterday, today and tomorrow, and unless even a few of us start to recast the mould that all of us are pressed very firmly into, then judgmentalism is here to stay. This is what kept and indeed keeps me going.

Practice

What I realised was that the only way I could practice was to maintain an awareness of my mission! If life got in the way and I stopped reflecting on this greater purpose, then it vanished. So, just like my little boy learning his times-tables, like my daughter learning how to make the perfect Chapatti, I knew that to get myself to a place where I had successfully re-wired my knee-jerk responses to more non-judgmental ones, I was going to have to just keep practicing. Eventually though, it began to work. I found it easier and easier to stop myself flicking the switch before blurting something out!

Candour

This was a big one. As discussed in chapter five, I learned that if I try to be as candid as possible with everyone about everything, regardless of how awkward the subject may be, it was actually one of the most liberating ways of engaging with my world. I say this because when we focus on talking straight with others, but also decide that we're going to be non-judgmental alongside being straight, it becomes the perfect combination to use when navigating ourselves through a conversation. When we reflect on the fact that to be candid is to be honest, we find much solace in the knowledge that it is a genuinely 'good' way of communicating. It also provides us with the kind of 'scaffolding' we need when working out those all-important momentary responses we have to give to another in any kind of interaction.

Conversations

This normally happens all by itself and it's quite natural too, when we discover something new to want to share it with others. The zeal and empowerment of newfound knowledge creates the fire in the belly, driving us to learn more and share more with others. However, as discussed above, the only way to sustain the transformation in ourselves and in others is to keep having the conversations about the new adventure. About our intentions, our failures, our successes as we inspire and motivate each other to make the change permanent, as opposed to a flash in the pan. Conversations also help us to improve what we're doing, constantly evaluating, tweaking, improving how we're doing it.

Apologies

One of the most difficult steps to take and indeed to keep taking was the act of admission. A candid and open apology to anyone of any age for anything I may have done wrong. Now to begin with, we're all essentially brought up to cower away from the thought of putting our hands up and saying, 'it was me…I was wrong.' This is very simply because a massive part of being judgmental is to find it utterly impossible to admit that we were wrong. Put another way, if ET were to land in my back yard and ask me what he needed to learn in order to be a successfully judgmental being, I would say one of his first priorities would be to learn how to, at all costs, avoid saying sorry for anything! 'why?' he would ask in his bleeping, popping, gurgling Martian tongue, 'well,' I would say, 'because it leaves you open to attack from the other person. You let down your guard. You become vulnerable. They can then point the finger at you. They become higher than you. More powerful than you, and above all, they get to say 'see, I was right all along, and YOU WERE WRONG!!! I'm better than you and you are a fool!'

However, I like to think that if I was indeed graced with a visit from a little green man from millions of light years away, and he wanted me to teach him, above all else, how to be judgmental, I would rather say 'look my very new friend, I could tell you to cover your ass as much as possible even if you're wrong and just attack attack attack the other person just so that they feel they can never point the finger at you again, but there truly is another, infinitely more beautiful way of going through life. That is to see the prospect of admitting your mistake as a way of actually making yourself more powerful, not weaker in front of the other person, and there are a few reasons why I think it's always best to admit where you were wrong:

1. It's actually less stressful for you to tell the truth, because you're not trying to make up lies. After all we all know that when we lie, we need to cover it with more lies. Things quickly get complicated; you'll end up forgetting one of the lies you told, and it will blow up in your face in more ways than one.

2. The other person is definitely not expecting you to do this. To put up your hands and say, 'you know, this was my fault.' It will throw them! They'll stand there, eyes glazed over, looking at you with a blank face. Why? Because they were ready for the lies, for the defensive, pre-emptive attack you were supposed to deliver on them, which would then have given them the excuse to make their own more severe counterattack and the conversation will have escalated into an all-out face-off of expletives. A 'fist fest' where both parties got to slog out all they had on each other until there was nothing left but damage!!!!!

3. By admitting you were wrong, you're actually demonstrating to the other person (especially if that other person is a child) that it's ok and good to do this. It's all about modelling the behaviour that you want to

see them showing. Your children will simply watch and learn. Dr Gottman has said in his book and in numerous lectures, that one of the most precious gifts we can give a child is an apology. Primarily because they get to see your vulnerable side as well as your authoritative side. However, they see that your vulnerable side is actually even stronger and more sincere than your authoritative side.

4. The act of apologising helps us so much to become humbler in how we see ourselves and the wrong deeds of others. I refer to the wrong deeds of others because when we become more prepared to acknowledge where we've gone wrong, we automatically become far more empathetic about others shortcomings. We see ourselves in their position, making the same or similar mistakes. It is a truly cathartic experience that delivers instant relief from the stress and anxiety of telling lies, as well as from our nagging conscience when we know we've screwed up. Life becomes a much more 'level playing field' between people because everyone is more prepared to acknowledge their mistakes in front of each other. That actually brings them much closer to each other, because they've both opened their emotional doors to each other and entered. They have gained massive respect for each other because their relationship has started to become based more on mutual love and care rather than 'tripping each other up.'

This idea of prioritising honesty and harnessing the sheer power in apologising to someone is one of the key principles to creating a non-judgmental world. I make this rather sweeping declaration because it seems crystal clear to me that in most confrontations, there are two potent things going on simultaneously and relentlessly:

The first one is our determination to be the one in the right, and it is because of this obstinate resolve that we are more than prepared to tell lies, or at the very least, should we say 'manipulate the truth a smidgen to get the upper hand in this game of wits.

The other force that is constantly looking to spring forth in the confrontation is our tendency to attack. Especially to make pre-emptive attacks and thereby prevent our opponent from any attacks they may be preparing to make. All this is unfolding as both combatants are in the 'fight or flight' state. All the defensive systems are on full alert and usually the very last thing we're willing to consider is throwing the towel in and apologising, when in reality, that is by far the easiest and most fruitful option for both parties.

I recently had a pretty disturbing conversation with an elder in my family, which quickly became an 'ear-bashing' from her. Someone from the older generation of traditional Pakistani immigrants here in England, who heard me apologise to my daughter because of the way I shouted at her. 'what were you thinking?!' she shouted at me. 'are you out of your mind apologising to a kid?!! All she will do now is think she's won!! She will not respect you! Don't you think you've now become weak in front of her?! You can't do that! You're the father! Fathers DO NOT say sorry to their kids!!!!!'

I did rather meekly ask her if she would like to see her grandchildren grow up having the courage to own up when they do wrong, to which she instantly said 'of course!' So I then even more meekly (if that can even be done) asked her how she thought that could possibly happen if nobody shows them how; when all they will see as they grow up are people who do not know how to acknowledge their mistakes. This response did not compute so she became defensive and I changed the subject, but it was a clear glimpse; a snapshot of how the vast majority of parents, carers, school staff, employers, line managers, CEO's, world leaders and mothers-in-law find it practically impossible to muster up the courage required to start apologising. I say 'start' because, just like any new territory we venture into, the first steps are always the hardest. It takes, I found real focus and commitment to start turning ourselves into more humble humans. Into people who find strength in owning up instead of weakness.

Forgiveness

Being active in acknowledging our mistakes in front of another encourages forgiveness on both sides. This is so so critical because we spend our entire lives hurting ourselves and others in some way shape or form. Many of us who assume the role of victim find and hold onto all the resentment, anger and enmity we felt against the perpetrator when they hurt us. This grip on our unforgiving judgmental side can even tighten, lasting our entire lives without allowing us to move on as well as taking nothing away from our 'wrong-doer.' From their perspective, they may have learned from their mistake and moved on. However, the victim finds a perverse and choking solace in tending to this flame of hatred. The satisfying knowledge that they (the victim) was right and their culprit was WRONG! All this time our victim wallows willingly in unhappiness in this prison of their own inability to forgive and move on. Stopping themselves from being truly happy. A 'bitter' pill taken steadfastly, once a day on an empty stomach.

The alternative? Forgive your culprit. Why? Because if they have in actual fact wronged you, a guaranteed punishment is the perpetual burden on their conscience that they have been carrying since they did the deed. A burden that they can never shed but only acknowledge to themselves and learn from. Believe me, our conscience always speaks the truth to us. It's our conscience making us flinch a little, whenever we remember or are reminded about what we did. This last sentence takes me with a jolt back to the now infamous, ill-famed BBC interview with our very own real life 'Grand Old Duke of York' Prince Andrew, who plays the very flinches, winces and shirking that I speak of here, while being questioned by a journalist on national TV. The man's guilt is as palpable as his indifference to the girls he has abused, but I still believe firmly that even Prince Andrew lives everyday with the burden of his dark deeds on his conscience.

You know, as much as I detest referring to Disney, I must say that never could Pinocchio have depended upon a more candid companion as his conscience

Jiminy Cricket.

As for the victim, once their culprit is made to face the law of the land for his or her misdeeds, they can only forgive if they want to move on and recover from the trauma. There is no other key to escaping their self-dug dungeon other than of course, popping out to the nearest purveyor of weaponry, acquiring a hand gun (with silencer) and pumping judgmental bullet after judgmental bullet into their poor sod of an un-suspecting culprit, who now in their later years, is probably kneeling down on their knee cushion trying to trim their rose bushes.

Nope! We've got to wake up to the fact that until we can release OURSELVES from resentment and bitterness about by-gone 'beef', we are, by our very own hand, impeding our own progress towards genuine and simple happiness. Each and every moment that passes in the 'state of hate' will not return again. It's gone, spent, wasted on the futility of our rage.

CHAPTER 8:
Just Follow The Conflict

You know, one of the most shocking realisations I had very early on in my research on Judgmentalism, was this:

That if you take a handful of the most significant issues and conflicts in the world, past or present, then attempt to trace them all back to their source, their terminus a quo, you will always find your old friend Judgmentalism, rearing his hideous head and looking back at you, smug but guilty as hell.

So let's have an identity parade of a few past and present scourges on society and put them to the judgmental test.

Slavery – Yep! On cotton plantations in America, rape and whipping of the slaves was routine. Just not done so much in front of other whites, and especially not the slave master's family. 'When I whip niggers, I take them out of sight and hearing of the house and no one in my family knows it.'

Apartheid – Check! Again, in colonialised South Africa, you could find big bill-board warnings everywhere for the white residents there that read 'CAUTION. BEWARE OF NATIVES!'

The Holocaust – Of course. Needless to say, when one man can order the deaths of around six million people, we know the human race and the problem of demonising others is a very serious one.

The Middle East crisis – That's an easy one! More of an industry that dates back to nearly 1,500 years than just a 'crisis' that appeared recently. It's all about people claiming the property of others as their own because they choose to believe that they are superior to their neighbours and being supported by others who have little or nothing to do with it.

Black civil rights movement – Absolutely! This is just one of the struggles by black people to deal with the fall-out from the 1862 Emancipation Proclamation drawn up by President Lincoln. The problem was and, clearly still is, that black people were continued to be demeaned and degraded across

American society, a society built on the blood and sweat of black slaves.

Racism – This is the big one. Racism has its origins reaching further back than most other conflicts in the world. So, we all know it's all to do with one person deciding to look down on another person because of their membership to another racial or ethnic group. Take the British Imperialism in India. It's a sunny day on August 24th, 1608, and a Proprietor of the London Based East India Company arrives in the city of Surat. He takes a look at the locals and decides that he, in his white tights and fake curly wig is better and more 'entitled' than they are. This act of unadulterated Judgmentalism results in the perfectly avoidable deaths from egregious deprivation of around 1.8 billion Indians. The company's racket was, apart from building and profiting from India's Opium trade, to export most of the food out of India, causing India's population to starve to death in the millions. In the East India Company's own hand-written daily logbooks, that are still in existence today, there are descriptions of dead bodies in the streets and the dying public resorting to cannibalism in order to survive. Judgmentalism has indeed led people to commit unspeakable evil against their fellow man throughout history.

This extremely dark chapter in human history is very much connected with me, as my parents were from the sub-continent. They were still children during the time of partition, when the British finally left India and Pakistan was born. However even now, whenever I travel to Pakistan, I see and hear the remnants of the colonialists in everything from the emphasis put on learning English in schools, through to architectural landmarks, sport, administration and communication. A pity this exchange of knowledge and innovation was merely a by-product of brutal and judgmental colonisation, instead of two different civilizations simply meeting and celebrating one another's rights and diversity.

I myself grew up in Black Country Dudley in the 1970's, so I was still only a nipper when, holding my mum's hand, I'd be strolling through Dudley Market place with her to buy fruit and veg. Now it seems obvious that both my mum and I were quite used to the racist abuse flung at us from passers-by pretty much constantly throughout our shopping trip. 'Oi you f***ing Paki!' 'Go back to your own country!' 'Black B*****d!' 'Coon!' 'Jungle-Bunny!' (some actually made me giggle!) We'd just look at the person, register what they were saying and then simply look away. It was just part of the territory when we were out and about. Part of the all too familiar noises and voices of a busy town centre. Again, at that time in 1970's Dudley, this was normal, so guess what…we treated it as normal! Didn't bother questioning it. It didn't even occur to us to report it either.

I recall a time in particular when we had boldly moved to where no other black or Asian family had moved before. A new housing estate called Withymore Village in Brierley Hill. As soon as we'd settled in, I found a large poster that had been left in our porch by some local residents. The poster had a really clever adaptation of the Ghost Buster movie logo where the image of a ghost is drawn within the prohibition sign (a circle with a line through it). However, clearly some local graphic design student had swapped the ghost for a bearded brown man wearing a turban! Beneath the logo were the words 'You move in we give you hell!' however, as usual, we were numb to it all. Didn't even bother reporting it, and we weren't given any hell either. Just a poster that fulfilled it's purpose of reminding me that I was born here, but this wasn't my home.

This was indeed the era in British history that saw a bizarre normalising of racial and sexual abuse. Through the culturally sinful hit TV sitcoms like 'Love thy neighbour', 'Mind Your Language' and 'It Aint Half Hot Mom' to the rise of 'Savillesque' TV/Media personalities who were somehow allowed to flourish, command the highest public respect and escape unscathed.

Extremism – Clearly based on judgmentalism. The whole definition of this is someone who has beliefs that most people think are unreasonable and unacceptable. This is mainly because these beliefs exclude and demonise anyone who doesn't accept and share them.

Domestic abuse – Another no-brainer for our identity parade. This is so predominantly made up of judgmental actions and words designed to dominate, belittle and damage another.

The Kashmir crisis – Definitely. The parting gift from Lord Mountbatten when the Brits left India was to draw a line on a map that would ignite a fire between two parts of the same people. This fire of conflict and hatred roars on to this day.

Sexism – Yes! This, the New Scientist magazine claims, began around 12,000 years ago when we became farmers. This gave birth to male dominance and ever since, the patriarchy of men judging women to be inferior, more fallible, weaker, and in the main, just there to bare children, look beautiful and give sexual pleasure, has and does continue to endure unabated, long after most farms have been concreted over!

The list unravels endlessly throughout history to prove time and time again that it's judgmentalism at the heart of all our problems. Name any others. Terrorism, class wars, political conflict, Inequalities in the workplace, self-harm, substance misuse, people trafficking, homophobia, the breakdown of the family unit or the environmental crisis.

Also, to be writing this in the wake of the public lynching of George Floyd and what followed and not make reference to its relevance, particularly to this chapter would be folly on my part. His death, like the deaths of probably millions of Black people in the USA since its inception, was yet another sobering example of how Judgmentalism can mutilate hearts and minds. How, a collective demeaning of a people over centuries can lead men to choose to needlessly take the lives of others, simply because of the colour of their skin.

I remember when I first caught sight of the mobile phone footage of the lynching. It was no more than a couple of hours after it happened. I was out in town, waiting in a socially distanced queue for a hardware store when it pinged into my phone.

As I watched it, I began to feel more and more nauseous as the victim's condition, lying on his front with such a weight pressing him down, was visibly slipping away. I could also feel the growing panic of the small crowd, as they too felt that what was unfolding did not need to be happening. That there were other options for those Police officers, but those present also clearly felt that if any of them were to advance forward to take matters into their own hands, things would have deteriorated much further. The ensuing riots, fuelled by President Trump's monumentally palpable hatred for Black people, were also just another notch on the wall of the American Black Historic struggle. I say this because things won't change unless people themselves do, and they will only change when they understand that they can and must.

Lastly, in this particularly grim and sobering chapter, we all owe it to the victims of what I can only describe as the worst kind of evil act, to acknowledge the depths of depravity that human beings can reach. These are the victims of sexual abuse, torture and murder and in particular, the global trafficking of children for this purpose. The customers for this massive industry are usually from amongst the top tier of society. politicians, world leaders, heads of law enforcement, top business personnel and even religious figures. The few victims who survive to tell of their experiences all describe the minds of these monsters as seeing their victims as essentially without value. They see themselves to be naturally superior and more valuable than the children they abuse or murder, so it is this grotesque and twisted judgmental detachment they create that allows them to justify performing these acts on children of all ages. Needless to say, that they were invariably subject to similar abuse themselves as children, so it duplicates itself; it plays out again on another child.

As a race of human beings and in particular of adults, we absolutely must wake up to the realities of what is happening right now, even as I write this, everywhere in the world. We must be courageous in confronting this truth in order to even begin to make it difficult for these gangs of men and women to run such repugnant rackets.

CHAPTER 9:
The 'How To' Chapter

After exploring the sobering realities of judgmentalism in our world, past and present, it's easy to become overwhelmed by the magnitude of its effects on us all, its potential to inspire the kinds of evil we have discussed in the previous chapter. It's these acts of evil against our own fellow man that really bring home how, throughout history, right up to this day, human beings have chosen first and foremost, to be judgmental, instead of any other alternative response. The reason we know, is that to be judgmental is, in the short term, easier. It's how we serve our ego and gain control of others. It's the first and most appropriate option for anyone setting out to do wrong and consider only themselves. Therefore, I think it's high time we got down to some brass tacks of exactly what it takes to be non-judgmental, because, put simply, it doesn't take a great deal. Only patience and a little perseverance initially as we train our obstinate brains to be more creative in their responses.

Now as I've explained several times already in this book, Emotion Coaching and the 5 steps that make up this simple and inspired way of dealing with people, falls perfectly in-line with non-judgmental behaviour. So, for this reason, the following two conversations are examples of when I have used the five steps to a, solve the problem and b, remain as non-judgmental as I possibly could.

Here's an example of how I've learned to use Emotion Coaching with my kids:

I was sat at my desk typing one evening and I could hear an argument unfolding between my daughter Maaria and my son Adam who were in the next room. I could hear that Maaria wanted to take her turn on the PS4, but Adam was refusing to let her. I could hear things escalating and eventually I heard a little scuffle before both kids started yelling at each other, bringing other arguments and insults into the verbal tennis match. Maaria then stormed out and sat down in the kitchen sobbing.

I walked into the kitchen then and could see she had that familiar 'livid' look on her face that I've seen on her mother's more times than I've had hot dinners. I already had an inkling that Maaria had probably resorted to trying to force the controller out of Adam's hands when he refused to play fair, but my priority was to hear it from her rather than start guessing. Here's how my conversation with her went:

Me: Hi darling, is everything OK with you?

Maaria: No. (She was looking down at the tabletop. Seething)

Me: Do you want to tell me about it?

Maaria: I'm really really angry with Adam! He's been on the PS4 for hours and now that I want a go on it, he won't let me! (She instantly raised her voice and said this with genuine desperation on her face.)

Me: Oh, ok. I could hear the argument and I even heard a bit of a struggle before you both started shouting at each other. What happened there?

Maaria: I wanted the controller dad, so when he kept refusing, I thought I'm gonna have to take it off him, so I went to grab it from him and he pushed me away! That's why we were shouting! Dad, when you bought the PS4 for us, it wasn't just for Adam was it?

Me: Of course it wasn't. It was for all of you. Well, I bet you felt quite frustrated when you knew it was your go and Adam still refused. (Maaria starts to nod her head and calm down)

Me: And when he pushed you, that probably made you feel even angrier with him.

Maaria: It did dad, and I fell back and hit my arm on the wall.

Me: Oh my goodness. Is your arm hurting now? Show me.

Maaria: It's fine dad but it just hurt when he pushed me.

Me: Ok. I'm glad you're feeling better now.

Me: You know what Maaria, I think I know exactly how you must be feeling right now. I remember this happening between me and my sisters all the time when I was your age. They used to know it was my turn when we were playing together but because they were bigger than me, they used to just ignore me. I remember feeling really helpless when that happened. (Maaria now is nodding her head again, agreeing with me.)

Me: But now that we've talked about how you felt, let's work together to think about a solution to this. So I completely agree with you that Adam was wrong to keep the controller in his hand and he should have given it to you, but do you think it made it worse when you tried to grab the controller from him?

Maaria: I suppose so...

Me: Ok, so what else could you have done instead of trying to grab the controller?

Maaria: Well, I suppose I could have told him that I'll speak to you or mum if he isn't listening. He knows that if you get involved, he will probably be banned from it.

Me: I totally agree. That would have been so much better than getting physical. And it would have avoided you getting hurt too. I'm going to speak to Adam too now about this, but what do you think you could do now to sort it out with him, especially so that it doesn't happen again with that controller.

Maaria: Me and Adam could make a chart that tells us whose turn it is and how long they can play on it. (Maaria instantly looks more positive and even a little excited about making a chart.)

Me: I think that's a perfect idea Maaria. Go for it, and before you do that I'll speak to him too.

Maaria clearly felt better. She had owned up to any wrong decision of her own as well as coming up with a realistic solution to the problem. She also felt closer to me because I had started by connecting with her first and discussing/accepting her feelings.

More importantly, she didn't feel like I had been judgmental, patronising or in any way made her feel like she had been 'the one in the wrong' or 'the stupid one.' It's really that simple, that with my help, she sussed it out herself, and the idea is that if I follow this process every time Maaria has a problem or Maaria is stressed, then eventually she will start to learn and believe that she is capable of problem solving independently. She will start to notice that every time she shares a problem with me, SHE is the one that, in the end, comes up with the solution, not her dad. This is the 'holy grail' of parenting I kid you not!!

I also feel it's important to share with you that when I first discovered Emotion Coaching, during the summer of 2015, my first thought was that surely Emotion Coaching could work between adult to adult too, and not only adult to child. You see, most of the practical examples given in the book portrayed scenarios between parent and child. This is the niggling question that drove me to make contact with the Gottman Institute, who, in no uncertain terms stated that they could only endorse what their scientific findings were based on (classic scientist behaviour), which was Emotion Coaching between adult and child. This didn't stop me. It was screamingly obvious that this would also work with the Mrs! I mean, it was all pressing the right buttons! Approaching her lovingly, asking what was wrong, jumping straight into getting on her side and empathising with her, then tackling the problem-solving bit at the end. It was a no-brainer! So, I waited for an opportunity to put it to the test, which came almost too quickly! She came in from work and I was in the kitchen preparing some food. She was visibly upset. She was letting off that kind of 'even if you dream of upsetting me, you'll need to wake up and apologise!' message through her body language and her tone of voice. It was my cue.

Me: Hi sweetie, how you doing?

Her: I'm fine (she sooo wasn't!)

Me: Are you sure? You look quite upset. Is everything ok?

Her: It's that manager again, I've just about had enough of him. You know, I don't know who the hell he thinks he is!

Me: Tell me what's happened darling. He's obviously really getting to you isn't he. Come and sit down. Do you want a cuppa?

Her: No, I don't. I just want to tell him exactly what I think of him! I'd rather not work at all if that's what I'm gonna be expected to put up with! I was late probably for the second time since I started at that crap hole and the way he spoke to me in front of the others was disgusting!

Me: Oh no, you know, I think that's the biggest mistake people make to have confrontations in front of others. It's the worst way to deal with anything. So, what exactly did he say to you?

Her: Well that was it. I was in the office with everyone and he just walked in and said 'you're late! And I've been waiting to get the Indus delivery sorted out, but I couldn't because you weren't here this morning!' You know, it was the way that he said it, literally shouting at me. I just can't believe how these people think it's ok to speak to anyone like that just because they're paying their wages!

Me: That must have made you feel so humiliated in front of the others and I mean, I know that you've hardly ever been late for work as well and actually, on most days you get to work early. It feels so unfair doesn't it when you know how much extra you give to your job, and then you get this in return. (She was now visibly calming down and nodding at everything I was saying.)

Me: You know exactly the same thing happened to me only last month at work when I'd just missed the deadline for submitting my scheme of work to the department head and in the staffroom, the way she spoke to me, I felt it was like she was speaking to one of the primary school pupils. I wished the ground could have swallowed me up. (She was nodding again and now she had calmed down completely, connecting with me because she felt that I was accepting how she felt as well as demonstrating that I had been through a similar experience to hers.)

Me: So, what are your thoughts on how to sort this out? Let's think about how you're going to resolve this because I really don't want you feeling uncomfortable going back into work because of this manager.

Her: Well, I would never do what he did. I'd never go in and give him a piece of my mind in front of others. It'll probably be a good idea to pull him to one side and speak to him. You know, he needs to know how embarrassed I felt when he just walked in front of everyone this morning.

Me: I think that's a perfect way to start sorting this out darling. By pulling him to one side, you'll be demonstrating to him how he should have done it in the first place. So what are you thinking you'll say to him? Do you think you should give him any explanation about why you were late?

Her: I suppose so, but it shouldn't really matter why I was late. The fact is that he simply didn't need to speak to me like that. I'm simply going to explain that to him, whether he accepts it or not.

Me: I agree, the best way is always to be honest and up-front with the other person. My guess is that when you do speak to him alone, he won't be expecting it, but he will appreciate you being so honest with him, and you might not believe it now, but it's often confrontations like these that actually end up making relationships better between people afterwards.

Her: Yeah. Maybe it will. (She had by now completely changed her expression from one of stress and anxiety to a look that told me a heavy weight had been lifted from her shoulders.)

Now there would almost be no point to this book other than simply spouting off my own take on judgmentalism that, I believe has gone largely un-checked by us the world over, if I didn't offer more practical examples of exactly what kind of responses we need to start adopting consistently in order to be more non-judgmental. I'm absolutely certain that by now in this book, you have a pretty clear idea of what our mission is and how we all need to start thinking whenever we find ourselves in a confrontational situation, or just at a time when we are asked to give our opinion on something or someone.

The above conversation with my wife is a simple enough example, but I'd also like to explore just some simple 'first responses' we could be giving instead of boring you to oblivion with whole conversations. This will be useful because I believe it's the initial response you give someone that is so often the trigger for a further escalation. It's that initial response, loaded with your 'fight or flight' knee-jerk outburst that feels great in the heat of that moment, until of course the other person takes their turn. The exchange of fire commences.

So below is a list of some of the most common scenarios that we encounter all day every day. Scenarios that invariably demand a judgmental response from us. You will see the judgmental response. Then, with each one, I'm also offering at least two alternative non-judgmental responses.

The idea behind this is to demonstrate just how straight forward the process of simple reflection and non-judgmental response is in such situations, and how the non-judgmental response can immediately diffuse the bomb.

Scenario 1

You are a manager at work and one of your members of staff has forgotten to send the post off on time because they were busy trying to complete the other tasks you had given them for the day.

Judgmental response:

'Jack, you know what time it is! You know that the post needed to be sent off before 4.30 otherwise we miss the last post at 5.30 and that means that all our customers get their orders a day later! You know it's because of carelessness like this from you that the reputation of the whole company goes down in all our customers eyes!'

Non-judgmental response 1:

'Jack, You've missed the last post for the customers' orders today, but I know you've been run off your feet with the tasks I gave you this morning. Let's work together to figure out a way to avoid this happening because we all know how much a late order upsets our customers.'

Non-judgmental response 2:

'Excuse me Jack, I've noticed we've missed the last post today. Is everything ok with you? You know, my responsibility isn't just to make sure everyone gets their work done on time. I will have failed in my job if I'm not making sure my staff are happy with the jobs they're doing. This is about everyone's welfare too. I'm always available for a chat if you need to discuss anything at all.

Scenario 2

A child is in a supermarket throwing a tantrum about wanting a toy that his mum can't afford. She would love to buy it for him, but she's already worried about not having enough for the rest of the shopping. He is shouting and demanding she puts it in the trolly.

Judgmental response:

'You are a naughty little boy Alex! There's no way that you're getting that toy with that horrible behaviour! Embarrassing me in front of all these people! Just you wait till you get home! I'm gonna....

Non-judgmental response 1:

Alex's mum takes him into her arms and gives him a hug. 'You really want that toy don't you Alex. It is a lovely car too with those 'go faster stripes' on it, and I can see how upset you're getting because you want it. The problem is that right now, if I buy the toy for you then we might not have enough money to buy the other things we need today. That's what I'm a little worried about. Imagine if we bought the toy today and then got home and you couldn't have that hot chocolate you love or the fruit juice, we all have with our breakfast.

Non-judgmental response 2:

Alex's mum takes him into her arms and says 'darling, you know the rule that if we want something then we always ask politely and we don't get angry if the other person says no for a good reason. You know that I don't have enough money for the toy today, but you're still getting upset. You know I really want to buy the toy for you as soon as I have enough money. Maybe tomorrow, so do you think that you can wait until then? We could plan our day tomorrow when we get home.

Scenario 3

A brother and sister are fighting over a bag of sweets. The brother pushes his little sister, who falls on the floor and starts to cry. A few minutes later his dad approaches him while he is eating his sweets.

Judgmental response:

I know what you did to your little sister! You're a bully! You should be ashamed of yourself! She's smaller than you! That's the last time I buy you any sweets!

Non-judgmental response 1:

I wanted to talk to you about you and your sister fighting over those sweets. I know that she was pushing you trying to get the sweets, but how do you think she felt when you pushed her so hard? Afterall, you are much bigger and stronger than she is.'

Non-judgmental response 2:

Can we talk about what happened between you and your sister? Do you think there was anything else you could have done instead of pushing her so hard?

Scenario 4

A woman is in a queue for a DIY store and she sees someone else pushing into the queue in front of her.

Judgmental response:

Oi! Can't you read the sign!? There's a queue here and you've just shoved your way in front of us!

Non-judgmental response 1:

Excuse me, you may not have noticed the sign, but the back of the queue is here.

None-judgmental response 2:

Excuse me, did you need to get in urgently? I thought maybe that's why you didn't join the back of the queue.

When we remember that there are always ways to convey our thoughts and feelings without being judgmental, we start to automatically and very consciously avoid any words that might trigger the other person.

Scenario 5

A couple are arguing about each other's families and one of them says 'I think your brother is a f***ing idiot!'

Judgmental response:

'Oh really, is that what you think? Well I think exactly the same about your sister! In fact, she makes my brother look like a saint!

Non-judgmental response 1:

You know the last time I spoke to my brother, he actually only had good things to say about you.

Non-judgmental response 2:

I am finding your words to be really hurtful. I'd really like to know why you feel that way about him.

Non-judgmental response 3:

I'm really worried about you. I'd like to help you find a way to sort this out with my brother. You know I'd be so happy if you could both work through these differences you've got.

Scenario 6

An elderly lady is spoken to quite rudely by a shop manager after asking for a refund.

Judgmental response:

How dare you speak to me like that! You are a rude man with no manners and none of the people skills you should have learned when speaking to your customers!

Non-judgmental response 1:

If it's ok with you, I'd like to offer you some feedback on the customer service I've received from your company. I was actually quite upset about the way you spoke to me and I felt it was important to tell you. Just because it might help you have a better approach next time.

Non-judgmental response 2:

I'd like to ask you a question if I may, and I'm not looking to upset you. I'd like to ask you how you think you might respond if you were in my shoes and a shop manager spoke to you the way you have just spoken to me. How do you think you'd feel?

Scenario 7

A teacher in a school receives a phone call from an angry parent who says "This is Jane Holden's mum! She told me this morning that Mr Raj singled her out after the science test for laughing out loud! I haven't brought her up to ever do something like that! It's you arrogant teachers who just make your minds up about a kid and then ruin their lives! You're all just bullies!"

Judgmental response:

I'm sorry Mrs Holden but you've got no right speaking like that to me! We don't come to work to be spoken to like that and if you're going to continue being rude then I'll just hang-up.

Non-judgmental response 1:

I'm really sorry that you feel like Jane has been treated unfairly Mrs Holden. You sound really stressed about it all, but you know, rather than get upset, the only way I can help you sort this out is if we can meet up. When are you free to pop into school?

Non-judgmental response 2:

Mrs Holden, I can hear how upset you are, so I'm going to focus on getting to the bottom of this with you. I really need to find out the facts first about why Jane was singled out, then I can come back to you with more information. I know how stressful these situations can be but if you can give me today, I'll speak to Mr Raj and to Jane so that we get a better idea about what happened.

From the scenarios above, we can see that firstly, the judgmental response will always run the risk of triggering a confrontation and this, unfortunately, is what we all see all day every day. Secondly, the non-judgmental responses are all designed to do exactly the opposite. Simply worded replies that want to de-escalate the situation. Furthermore, they want to set out immediately on the road to finding a solution without appearing to be feeble or un-assertive. This is the power of a non-judgmental response to a judgmental one. Its sole purpose is to keep both parties calm, connecting and co-operative but still aware of each other's rights and positions. To be non-judgmental is by no means to come across as feeble or lacking in the conviction to solve a problem.

The other very powerful effect of someone giving a non-judgmental response is that the recipient suddenly sees them as being a lot more in control of the situation. The non-judgmental party is suddenly navigating the dialogue, pulling back the reins of the confrontation and re-setting the pace to a steady trot. At this pace, it's so much easier for both sides to focus on problem solving than defending themselves. There's even a moral upper hand that the non-judgmental speaker generates as he/she was the one to first take the initiative, calm themselves down and demonstrate how it's done.

It's quite beautiful. I have met some people in my life who have displayed this kind of humility and readiness to be more of a help than a hindrance. People who are not always in search of ways to trip others up, but people who actually look so at peace with themselves that, to approach them and strike up conversation feels natural and effortless. One does so with the knowledge that whatever they say to this individual, it will be listened to with an open and sincere mind.

Also, one of the most remarkable things about these humble humans is that when they speak, their voice is seldom loud. In fact, because they're known as a person of few words, when they do speak in a low voice, those around them will invariably lean forward and listen far more intently to what they have to say than, say, me! I'm a little louder.

CHAPTER 10:
The Non-Judgmental Revolution
Should So Completely Be Televised!

So, I believe quite simply that we are all expected to be judgmental without having a clue about how easily we could learn to stop it. There is blatantly a conflict of interest in the minds of those powers that be. The short-sighted governments and multi-national corporations, manufacturers of all goods and devices that are so carefully built not to last or fade as quickly out of fashion as they appeared! For a judgmental society is a society that hungers for all the material wealth that they purvey on our TV screens, billboards, cinema trailer ads, magazines and social media platforms, oversaturated with compulsion to spend all we have for the latest whatever.

The most expensive 'prime-time' slots of TV, when the media machine has its captive audience's undivided attention, are snapped up by the big retailers. Imagine being able to use even a few of those slots to connect with the people, to convey messages that are less about the 'goods' we chase and more about the 'good' we unwittingly yearn.

Judgmental is how we survive, how we get what we want, how we size someone up, how we dominate others, how we calculate our next move in life, career, friendships, romance and the rest.

Judgmental is the reason why we're so desperate to out-do each other in such wealth, displaying all our latest consumer acquisitions or holiday destinations on our social media pages, another milestone reached ahead of the rest in the great and futile rat race. Changing our faces and bodies to emulate 'the beautiful,' subscribing with such un-questionable complicity to the disparity between the haves and the have nots in the world today.

'The World Counts.com' declares that 'If Earth's history is squeezed into one year, the modern human has existed for 37 minutes and used up a third of Earth's natural resources in the last 0.2 seconds. On climate change they warn us all that 'the threat of abrupt and irreversible climate change is growing. There is an increasing consensus that critical tipping points are approaching after which global warming will be impossible to stop. The loss of the Greenland and

West Antarctic ice sheets would cause sea levels to rise 10 meters. This could happen already in this century.' All of these factors are fuelled by the force of judgmentalism. Of a decision WE make that WE are more entitled than someone else.

There are even many amongst us who will declare that to be judgmental is one of the most basic instinctual elements of any human being. It is, for better or for worse, part of who we are as fallible beings. Beings that are born and bred to focus on 'me.' Tied to the self. An inability to relinquish a grip on the self and open up to the notion that we are each an individual part of the whole. This is why the balance between ourselves and our relationships with others is, with the growing complexity of our time, tipping gradually towards 'number one.' A productive start if exploring number one was all about learning and growing in order to share oneself with others, the feelings of others, the vulnerabilities of others, the potential in others. However, I hold the firm belief that human beings everywhere have the potential, the power to choose alternative responses to responses that trigger conflict. Every one of us can be taught to step back, be creative in how we respond and solve problems with others instead of provoking and clashing.

This leads me to Imagine, Just for a moment, a time when our global institutions like the UN or the EU were to wake up to the dire need and indeed the sheer potential for change in our world; if they put combatting judgmental behaviour at the top of their 'to do' list. If they announced that, 'there will now commence a phased effort on the part of all governments, to educate our people about the devastating impact of judgmentalism on their lives and the support we all need to curb this age old paradigm. This will be an effort for change that will begin in certain parts of our society first, where it is needed most, before then broadening to the whole of society.'

This wishful notion that the world takes up metaphoric arms against judgmentalism sparks yet another rather interesting question. A question that could indeed inform how and where, in our communities, we would need to start in spreading the knowledge and support about Judgmental behaviour, if we really were to begin today. One would suddenly feel like they were standing in the middle of a 'serial hoarder's living room the size of a football pitch, tasked with the responsibility of tidying the place up! The simple fact that judgmental behaviour permeates through every part of our lives, three hundred and sixty degrees, makes this challenge even more, how should I put it, interesting!!

So, when we venture forth into the centre of the judgmental minefield of our communities, we may need to start by reflecting on who in society we should start with. Who could be the most powerful transmitters for our message, through whom we could spread the word? Well, I think it's all about us first clarifying what our intention is. What is it that we want to achieve here? Now for an issue of this scale, I was convinced that whatever the intention was, it would need to be a realistic one. An achievable one. Afterall, if we set ourselves targets we can't achieve right from the start, then the revolution is doomed even before it has begun.

It's at this point, completely out of the blue, as is so often the case, that the words 'humble humans' popped into my head. Two words that tumble off the tongue, arm in arm with such beauty, and two words that felt like they just said it all. People who have humility. Is that not what we should all be striving for? Because surely humble humans are the people that everyone levitates towards; feel most at ease with. Humble humans are those individuals least troubled by affairs of the ego, of needing the attention and praise of others. They are also very naturally the least judgmental people you will ever meet. Now I must say that as I repeated that pair of words over and over in my head, I came pretty close to changing the title of this book! 'well you bloody well should have!' I can almost hear you mumble. But I didn't.

So getting back to creating humble humans everywhere. How do countries, communities, neighbourhoods make that gradual transition from judgmental ones to non-judgmental ones? I believe only an oxymoron can put it best. That the answer is as simple as it is challenging. Our transmitters are obviously the adults amongst us who must wake up first. We must first acknowledge together that on our current trajectory, we will continue to replicate and proliferate the same blunders, the same retrograde steps in how we engage with each other and our planet that we've been taking for centuries. As acknowledged earlier in this book, I feel that there is a growing awareness in people about emotions, about how scientific knowledge of how our feelings impact our health and life outcomes has taken leaps and strides. However, all this knowledge and research is little more than a dumb, un-thumbed textbook sat gathering dust on a bookshelf until it is shared with people from all walks of life and in all corners of the globe.

This is about making knowledge accessible, stimulating and exciting to all, not just the few. About inspiring people to reflect and then change. The 'grown ups' must change, then the children will follow. In order for there to be sustained and embedded change in how we respond to each other, we must develop our own capacity first. When our children are exposed to non-judgmental behaviour, then they will grow up too, wired for a non-judgmental life. Logic dictates that our children will simply watch and learn. Over and above their initial personality 'blueprint' that they were born with, we know that the behaviours our kids display are learned from those around them.

So the lightbulb moment every parent/carer needs desperately to have right now everywhere is the realisation that their actions and words are being seen and heard, not just occasionally, but constantly, through every crisis, confrontation and mundane situation they find themselves dealing with, and our kids and their brains are taking in data from all of these, both positive and negative experiences.

These are the children that we so often see being excluded from mainstream schools because of emotional behavioural difficulties. These are the children who are regularly ill through spending so much of their lives in that 'fight or flight' state. These are the kids then that quite naturally start to use drugs, get involved in crime in their community, then inevitably join the prison population.

It brings me back to one of my favourite quotes of all time about the kids we've been given the almost divine responsibility and indeed privilege to educate. American author Barbara Coloroso said 'when kids come to us from strong, healthy, functioning families, it makes our job easier. If they do not come to us from strong, healthy, functioning families, it makes our job more important.'

These are also the kids that get diagnosed with the American-made spectre of ADHD (Attention Deficit Hyperactivity Disorder), another racket that flies in the face of anything decent, fair or humane in our world. This 'condition' was, without any doubt, conceived around a pharmaceutical company board room table by already overpaid executives being paid and promised even more to come up with 'new ideas that will bring in more revenue,' and just like so many predatory pursuits enjoyed by the great powers of this world, it was specifically designed to target the poor. In this case, the children of the poor.

Now there will be many amongst you who are unfamiliar with this condition and its treatment and that's because your kids are pretty much normal. Apart from, of course, the judgmental side to all of us, many kids, even if they are more mischievous or lively than other kids, will never have the ADHD stamp on their foreheads. No, the kids that get that stamp are mostly the troubled kids from the lowest socio-economic neighbourhoods. The kids that we just talked about, that spend very unhappy, unstable childhoods filled with separating parents, verbal/physical abuse, poverty and to top it all, no role-models to show them the potential each and every one of them have inside.

ADHD is the sinister remedy for kids that we can't, or rather, don't want to have to manage or engage with in any meaningful way. The official symptoms of ADHD are inattentiveness, hyperactivity and impulsiveness which are incidentally the classic, historic symptoms of a child who is unhappy, traumatised and neglected. This adds up perfectly because the majority of kids diagnosed are from deprived neighbourhoods and broken families. So why are we not connecting the dots?

Once a doctor diagnoses a child with ADHD, the child is usually put on pills that, our pharmaceutical executives claim, help the child to concentrate better, be less impulsive, learn and practice new skills and overall, feel calmer. Now, if I hadn't spent the last twelve years working with these children and families, I would never have seen the reality of a child who is ordered to take these drugs on a daily basis, especially and tragically on school days. On the days that that child needs more than ever to be in control of their faculties, be ready to learn and engage, be active and alive. When the doped-up child arrives in school, they are anything but ready to learn new skills. In their eyes and their whole demeanour there is a dumbing down. They are visibly not all there. Yes indeed they are calm and perhaps less impulsive which clearly makes their behaviour easier to manage, however what vanishes while the drugs are in effect, is the child; the vitality, the excitement, energy and unpredictability that is such a beautiful part of watching our kids grow and learn. I cannot count the number of slurred conversations I've had with children who are sick of taking pills that leave them 'comatose' as so many of them have put it.

It's painfully clear who the so-called winners are behind ADHD. Government and big pharma, who stand to reap profits from their newly invented condition, the parents who, through a diagnosis can claim extra benefits for managing their child and the school who would much prefer the dumbed down version of Jack than the one that's more of a challenge to manage, taking the pressure off their staff and their attendance/performance figures. To hell with Jack and any potential that lies dormant inside him.

It is also an uncanny coincidence that the day I'm writing these thoughts on ADHD, one of my greatest heroes and a powerful critic of ADHD, the Educator Sir Ken Robinson has died at the age of 70. In Sir Ken's world-famous TED speech delivered in 2006, now the most viewed TED speech since the launch of the platform, Sir Ken refers to ADHD as a condition that was 'invented.' He gives a powerful example of a young girl named Gillian Lynne in a 1930's school who just couldn't sit still and whose helplessly judgmental parents and school thought she may have a learning disorder. They had no idea what to do. Gillian

Gillian was just always springing around everywhere, never handed in work on-time and nobody seemed to be able to pin her down. eventually she, along with her mum was sent to see a Specialist. In the meeting, the specialist spent some time in front of Gillian, going over the problem with her mum. He then told Gillian that he would need to speak with her mum alone. Now as they left the room, the specialist turned on his radio, to which Gillian immediately got up and started dancing. The specialist asked her mum to take a look through the door saying 'Mrs Lynne, Jillian isn't sick, she's a dancer.'

Sir Ken remarks that if ADHD had been 'invented' back then, Gillian Lynne would have been put on 'dumbing down' medication and would have never become the world famous dancer and choreographer that she is now. His career's principle argument was that 'schools kill creativity.' He argues that since the Industrial Revolution, the world has been more concerned with producing kids that are more academic than creative. It's completely true, if our kids are great at literacy, numeracy and the sciences, then they are readily classed as 'intelligent.' They are seen as the ones who will go far in life. All of those who don't fit this mould, on the other hand, are 'unintelligent' and will spend their lives struggling. The irony is that it's the creative thinkers amongst those kids that are the greatest contributors to mankind. The innovators. The individuals whose legacies resonate far beyond their short lives.

I believe this paradigm has ruthlessly limited the development of our children, in so many cases, sabotaged their futures, and ultimately deprived all of us of countless 'game-changers', geniuses, visionaries and prolific leaders.

And yet again, we find the 'baddie' of our book at the root of all this. Judgmental thought and behaviour is all that's needed to vitiate the progress of anything, anytime, anywhere. When we are all going to wake up to this bloody fact is anyone's guess!

It is at this point that we need to become aware; we feel the enormous weight of our responsibility to our kids. Of our responsibility to be acutely conscious of the words and actions we play out in their presence. For it is these words and actions that they take in, process and respond to, and the effects of these experiences will manifest themselves in countless ways for countless years to come. We are their first school, their world, their concept of 'normal,' so to be complacent in this work is a dereliction of duty. A denial of our kid's right to a fair, loving and balanced start to their life. Moreover as parents/carers, we should never fear our inevitable screw-ups either, as long as our kids see that we're prepared to acknowledge those screw-ups, learn something from them and move on. In fact, one of the most precious lessons for our kids is when they see how we deal with a mistake. A priceless opportunity for them to see that mistakes are actually more powerful opportunities for humility, learning and development than causes for anxiety, depression and finger pointing. Our mistakes and the lessons we learn from those, especially our power to poke fun at ourselves afterwards are, I believe, more productive than our successes.

I think what we're looking at here are some of the main ingredients for raising a whole generation of children who are resilient both emotionally and physically, and who above all else, are quite used to communicating non judgmentally with their world. They will have grown up learning, right from their early years, non-judgmental responses to all of their everyday scenarios with family, friends, classmates, school staff and community. That's because the non-judgmental revolution will have started with its kids, and all who are the stakeholders around our kids? Their parents or carers and their school staff. These are therefore our first 'transmitters.'

This is the 'sea change' we're looking for because this is where we will have steered the trajectory of a whole generation (and countless generations after) of our children towards a more non-judgmental society. A society that, step by step, generation by generation will shift from the conflict we see and experience around us everywhere today, to communities filled more and more with empathy, love and diversity. It is this alteration of a family's negative outcomes to positive ones that I have witnessed first-hand. When I worked with the families of young people who had been excluded from mainstream schools, I saw that many of these parents/carers had all been through the same process too of exclusion and referral to an alternative provision like a PRU. So, the pattern was inter-generational and, all these families fully expected future generations to follow suit too. Afterall, that's the way it had always been. Until of course I began to show the parents ways to manage their child's behaviour. Ways that instantly began to give them more power and a stronger connection with their child. That's when their behaviour and their child's behaviour started to change along with the whole culture of their home life. I continued to catch-up with these families after the support sessions and found, to my utter delight, that most of them had maintained some very positive changes in their lives and relationships. Thus, the trajectory of negative outcomes for these families had indeed been altered. How much exactly is not clear, but there had been remarkable progress that these parents had never seen before.

You know, I say this to many many people I meet about the sheer possibilities in changing people's thinking for the best. I say that by changing the thinking of one parent and child, by sharing knowledge with them that inspires them to adopt new approaches in their lives and start to progress, you are potentially and inevitably transforming the outcomes of numerous future generations of that family from negative to positive ones too. The snowball (Almost Back to The Future) effect of your intervention is incalculable as it resonates on into that family's future.

Ok, so it certainly makes sense to begin with children and families, along with the school staff that will work with them, but who else should be next on the 'priority list' of the non-judgmental revolution? Well, if we reflect on which professionals in society need more soft skills to do their jobs, skills like dealing with people judiciously and empathetically, we think of medics, lawyers, politicians, police, social workers, youth workers, sales people, managers/supervisors and HR personnel to name just a handful. These are the People who, as part of their profession, are faced with social/medical problems to solve, confrontations, complaints, grievances and organisational/logistical challenges. Only when we begin to list non-judgmentalism's beneficiaries do we start to see the sheer scope of the work to be done.

CHAPTER 11:
A Reverie Of The Future

After exploring this single three syllable word, I can honestly say that even when I began this book, I had little idea that its significance was actually this great. That it pervaded not only all nations but also all spheres and levels of life. That whether our dwelling is a slum or a palace, we are equally slaves to its allure and its demands. So for the first time in my life, during these hours, days, weeks and months granted to me by the double-edged sword that is the lockdown, I have realised the power in investing one's time, energy and thought into one thing. Something that perhaps others haven't reflected upon to this extent, or maybe have but just not acted upon it. Not tried to put it down on paper and initiated a discussion.

The writer may well think at the outset that they are an empty vessel, and indeed I believe they're not far wrong. However, (and by now you know I choose my words carefully) a miracle starts to happen as they think, because as they think, they write, and as they write, they think, and as this process takes flight, so do their ideas cavorting and soaring into directions that this solitary thinker had never previously imagined. The empty vessel just goes on relentlessly pouring fourth its contents. Contents that have simply appeared from the grey matter and all its infinitely secret pathways, summoned up and given life on the page.

This has been my journey, of simply watching the mind-map in my head of the ground I know I must cover in this book, explode perpetually until it reaches its natural end. To this end, I can't express enough how urgently we all need to embark on our own journeys. Journeys that allow us individually to reflect deeply on something in our lives and to know it. Then, through our creative power, breathe life into these thoughts, so that they can be shared with everyone.

It's these thought processes that compel and excite. That continue to play out as we now start to visualise what our non-judgmental world might look like.

Many of us know the importance of visualisation and how it assists us in maintaining focus on where we want to be, and, given a human beings capacity to imagine what could be, I've been looking forward to this chapter in rather a big way.

So, when we begin by considering the game-changing effects of people everywhere in the world becoming less judgmental, the landscape in our heads actually starts to take on quite a utopian feel. Now, I'm fully aware of anybody's tendency to start 'seeing things through rose tinted spectacles' when imagining something they want as badly as I want a non-judgmental planet, but even when I factor this in, the vision in my mind is still a beautiful one. The reason for this is that the very plausible changes that will happen in people when they simply start to alter their responses to each other everywhere really will completely transform our world.

People will fight less, and problem solve together more. This will be everywhere, in the home, the workplace, at the supermarket, on the street. So, crimes in these places will reduce. The eye-wateringly high prison budgets everywhere will plummet along with crime levels making our neighbourhoods safer.

Needless to say, 'Big Pharma', the global corporate monsters that have made trillions and stand to make yet more from 'the great pandemic' will actually start to quake in their Tom Ford custom shoes too. Because the fact is that the health of the world's population will flourish. Just the nosedive made by the annual Cancer treatment revenues alone will stop these corporations and their investors in their tracks.

Levels of depression and mental illness will also go down, and as a result, substance abuse of all kinds will do the same. Why? It's simple! Because people will be happier, and when they're happier, they're healthier, more relaxed, more creative and therefore more productive across the board. We are all under no illusion at all that when we're happier, we're much less likely to develop serious, terminal illnesses. Dysfunctional lives will start to heal, and children will start to grow up in a very different world to the one we know now, because for starters, much less of these children will be in care. They will start to thrive because their emotions and behaviours will be managed in very similar non-judgmental ways in both school and home and as we all know, kids thrive on consistency.

Also imagine a law-enforcement system that's based on being non-judgmental. Now I hasten to clarify something here that we explored much earlier in the book. That to be judgmental is simply to be over-critical. To pass unfair judgment because, in that moment, that's what we wanted to do. Like the officer who decided not to lift his knee off the back of George Floyd's neck, or the lawyer who was getting paid handsomely to defend and support a known paedophile and sex offender. If our law enforcement system consisted of non-judgmental people, then the whole institution would command the respect it should earn from the public it serves and protects. Just like school staff, hospital nurses, social workers and prison officers, a police officer, trained to use more non-judgmental and empathic behaviour will always be more skilled in handling a volatile, potentially life-threatening situation than an officer who hasn't had such training.

With employers and leaders receiving the right mandatory training and support, people's emotional wellbeing in their jobs and in the community would start to thrive. Politicians would spend more of our hard-earned cash on thinking of solutions rather than political arm twisting, corruption and spitting judgmentalism at one another. World leaders would truly start to become the judicious, selfless and empathetic individuals we have always needed them to be.

From an environmental perspective, it's simple to deduct that as humans become progressively and naturally more non-judgmental with each other, their take on the planet that sustains us all would also be reformed. Now, it is clear that activism for environmental change is alive and well. There are numerous organisations doing amazing work for this cause in every continent. However, what is also alive and well is the spectre of global industry, like the livestock industry or the car industry that thrive unabated. So, if we took these two industries alone and viewed them through our rose-tinted revolution spectacles, we probably wouldn't even recognise them. Take the livestock industry. I believe less judgmental folk would be less obsessed with packing meat into their diets. Now as far-fetched as this may sound, my feeling is that to be a fully-fledged carnivore requires a certain amount of apathy on the consumer's part. Apathy and in many cases repugnance and even disgust when they're asked to witness the slaughter of the young lamb, they delightfully munch through for Sunday lunch. That's primarily because the methods used in the mass production facilities for meat leave a hell of a lot to be desired in terms of how the animals are reared and then slaughtered, and the fact that we, the mass population allow this to go on unabated is also rooted in our judgmental superiority complex over the animal kingdom. I mean, we've never flinched at lording it over each other, so we shouldn't really expect to lose sleep over 35,000 chickens crammed together in a shed for their whole, very short lives in complete darkness. As the retail meat industry grows exponentially to 'meet' this demand, the packaged body parts of meat we throw into our shopping trolleys couldn't look any less like the animal they were sliced off.

Another shocker for me was the discovery that about three quarters of all the agricultural land in the entire world is used only for the livestock industries like meat, dairy, egg and fish farming. The official figure given on the compelling Netflix documentary 'Game Changers' is 83%, however by using 83% of the planets farmland, we're only getting about 14% of the worlds calories. The majority of the calories we all need every year come from plant-based food. Again, I link these statistics to our age-old stagnant habits of being stuck in our old ways. The archaic, gluttonous myth that 'guys need meat to be real guys!' and all it is is a hubristic refusal to take on new ideas and new perspectives, even when faced with new scientifically, technologically proven research.

So generally, a less judgmental world be one that invests far more into improving how we breed, rear, treat and slaughter the animals we so desperately want to eat. It's a given that meat would be more expensive because producers would rightfully be spending more on their product. This would only encourage us to eat less meat and turn more to what modern science claims is our natural choice of diet. A plant based one. The environment wins and so do we. That 83% of all our agricultural land would be reduced dramatically, freeing up land for more plant-based food production as well as construction to house a now thriving population.

The car industry too is another gleaming, chrome plated example of people demanding the vulgar in order to 'large it' over others who can't afford it. The phallic status symbol gone utterly bezerk. Now I'll be as fair as I possibly can under the circumstances when I pay homage to the undeniable contributions the car industry has made to iconic design as well as to innovations in comfort and fuel efficiency, but that's as far as I'm going in favour of the great four wheel racket that inflicts numerous injuries on us and our green earth.

So, before we put on our rose-tinted spectacles, let's consider what these injuries are. Well, firstly there is the threefold impact on our environment from the colossal car industry. That is the energy and resources needed along with the pollution from our unsatiable hunger to make them, then to run them, and then inevitably to dispose of them.

Secondly, cars have and continue to make us lazy, unfit and overweight. Before experiencing my worst bout of Sciatica, then splashing out on my first mountain bike a few months ago, (which completely cured my pain and gave me cardio strength that I've never had before) I had spent years using the car even for trips to the corner shop on my street! I'm now looking for excuses to leave the car at home and peddle my way to wherever I need to go. The satisfaction of knowing I've made it from A to B without burning any fuel, using the strength of my own legs and getting stronger for it, is, alone, reason enough for governments everywhere to follow the example of countries like Denmark, China or Finland. Denmark's capital Copenhagen is known as the city of cyclists where 52% use a bike for their daily commute. Needless to say, cyclists are far healthier generally than car users. But Copenhagen is way ahead of most other cities in the world, where people have to campaign like mad for dedicated cycling lanes on roads because the priority is given to cars, to getting there fast and saving time. The irony being that it's cyclists who can end up living longer, healthier lives by just slowing down a little and using 2 wheels instead of 4. So, in our non-judgmental world, the bicycle reigns supreme! Lastly, about cars versus bicycles, when asked if I had to choose which of these I would rather get hit by, I'm pretty sure I'd prefer the one that weighs kilos and not tonnes!

This is just part of the backdrop to the gleaming bodies and hand-stitched interiors of our car industry that, just like the meat industry, gives testimony to our fixation with judgmentalism. To our desire to 'out-do the Jones's.' Being the one with the latest car feels a lot like being the one in the right!

But why? I believe it's as plain as a pikestaff and we discussed this earlier in the book too. We're taken back to the association people make to the 'haves' and the 'have nots' in our world. An association that looks to affirm that those who 'have' are somehow more superior, more entitled, even more 'favoured' by the good Lord than those who don't.
It is this social dynamic, this prerogative that our governments and the worlds super wealthy elite (the infamous 1%) want us focussed on. An appetite for more and more that only bolsters the hold of judgmentalism on all of us in every part of our lives and brings them dividends like never before. It feeds our world economy with individuals, communities and corporations falling over each other just to make more, to own more, to profit more, to eat more, to boast more, to show more, whilst giving the bare minimum.

I can see the egocentric ambitious drive, the hunger for material wealth and success that most parents actually mis-spend their lives trying to nurture in their children far too much. I think most of us do it. I've got four kids and I catch myself perpetrating the same. Investing a lot more of the time I have with my kids on preparing them for a life of 'earning' and 'hoarding' but nowhere near enough on 'giving and knowing themselves.' Why? Because the machine commands it. 'The man' commands it! Our fears and insecurities of 'running out' drive us and our kids into the rat race starting gate even before we've started high school. Our plans/aspirations and coaching of our kids seem to go like this:

Focussed school study/don't you get in with the 'wrong crowd! I only want you mixing with the students in the 'top sets!'= the best exam grades = the best job/business = Money and power = happiness, stability, respect, admiration and the envy of others. To hell with everything else. 'Keep your eye on your own ball because nobody else is going to do it for you.'

The flip side through our magic spectacles? Parents who are bringing their children up to understand the critically important balance they must have between their own needs and their society's needs. Parents who are putting at least as much emphasis on teaching their children the 'soft-skills' they will need, the emotional intelligence it will take to deal with all of life's challenges in the most positive, resilient and responsible way they can. The simple fact that the children will have been brought up using more non-judgmental, empathic behaviour will do most of the work for us.

We've also already looked at the current state of our faith communities in terms of the clear presence of judgmental behaviour where actually there should be none. So again, I can't resist imagining how different the faith sector of our societies might look if all faith groups began to eradicate this disease. Well, for starters, faith organisations wouldn't be run like giant corporate empires that own vast swathes of real-estate, property and businesses across the globe. They would, by their very 'divinely 'prescribed nature, be infinitely simpler organisations, there and only there to serve their flock as well as the wider community.

Just like the mandatory training we're proposing be given to all other leaders of businesses, large and small and all leaders in the public sector, faith leaders too would be subject to this training legislation. Training and support that instils in them the qualities they know they need, like real piety, humility and an appreciation of all other faiths. Most importantly, the skills they need to connect with all people of all ages and backgrounds.

This, then is the world where we would actually have woken up to see the great duplicity of our leaders and the now all powerful, all knowing media/marketing industry? A world where, as a human race, we would have started to wise up to what's more important to us than our bank balance if we are to become a more peaceful and loving planet.

This would be a world where again, just like 'big pharma', the great purveyors of material wealth, the corporations would finally start to loosen their hold over us. A dead-tight grip that dictates ours and our children's desire for more and more would give way to people everywhere meeting, at long last, their inner selves. People beginning to understand what was always more important than the race. Their relationships, their rights, their health, their planet and, standing next to each other, their astonishing, beautiful diversity.

I'm certain, therefore, that our lives would become much simpler, without having to compromise on innovations in technology, scientific research, creative thinking or our role in environmental conservation. Simpler, simply because our priorities would shift from the superficial and selfish, to the meaningful and selfless. Wealth would be far more equally distributed, a playing field levelled out and inclusive for 'all creatures, great and small', regardless of their background, the colour of their skin or any other excuse we seem so desperately to need in order to lord over each other.

Judgmentalism encompasses all of our worlds social, economic ills. It is what we find each and every time we trace any issue back the root. This is why a non-judgmental approach to how our world is run, to how we tackle key issues in every part of society, and to how we prioritise creative thought, would be the cataclysmic turning point we all need to take back control at a time where right now, in the 'Covid-19 world', we are losing faster than ever.

Acknowledgements

Shamsa Aslam, Khadijah Aslam, Aisha Aslam,
Adam Aslam, Maaria Aslam, Dr Zareen Ahmad,
Naurin Ahmed, Saiqa Ehsan, Tehsin Aslam,
Sohail Aslam, Hazel Pitt, Dr Janet Rose,
Shayan Ehsan, Jillian Terry, Richard Koenig,
Andrew Higginbotham,
The Halimah School of Excellence in Pakistan.

About the author

Rohail Aslam

Author, Artist & Teacher, Rohail graduated from Liverpool University in the early 90's and after several years in London, returned to his home town of Dudley in the West Midlands. Here, he began teaching Art and English in the community, with children and young people with Emotional Behavioural Difficulties. However Rohail became increasingly interested in exploring the paradigm of inter-generationally challenging behaviour in all age groups. An issue faced by all communities but particularly present in more deprived parts of society. He could see that in order to change the behaviour of a child, we need to first change the behaviour of the adults responsible for that child. The parents and the school staff. In 2015 Rohail set up a Community Interest Company ACTOV Change to begin more focussed work on supporting parents in learning more about how to engage with their children. It was at this point that Rohail discovered the work of Dr John Gottman of the Gottman Institute in the US. Their research on Emotional Intelligence transformed his work with families and organisations in all sectors.

However, it wasn't until the start of the Covid-19 lockdowns and the disturbing rise in domestic violence worldwide, that Rohail began to look further. An attempt to understand why people everywhere of every age, socio-economic level and nationality were so used to the idea that a disagreement should always begin with a blow-out. That the first priority is always to speak before we think, to vent the anger, to do the damage, to 'win the argument' before we even think about picking up the pieces afterwards. This is what led Rohail to explore Judgmental behaviour. For it was clear that it is our propensity to be judgmental that leads to conflict of any kind any time, anywhere. It was also clear to him that if people everywhere could be supported in learning more non-judgmental behaviour, the world could start to look very different indeed.

Rohail now delivers both online and face-to-face Non-Judgmental Response Training to families, school staff and employers in the UK and abroad. He continues his practice as an Artist and to teach Art to children with emotional behavioural difficulties. He lives with his wife and four kids in the Black Country.

Notes

Notes

Notes